Sunset

Bookshelves
& Cabinets

By the
Editors of
Sunset Books
and
Sunset Magazine

Lane Publishing Co. ▪ Menlo Park, California

Echoing the ceiling lines, whimsical zigzag uprights brace maple rails in this bookshelf unit. Tempered safety glass shelves sit in rabbets in the 1-by rails. Design: Osburn Design.

Book Editor
Scott Atkinson

Contributing Editor
Susan P. Warton

Coordinating Editor
Suzanne Normand Mathison

Design
Joe di Chiarro

Illustrations
Bill Oetinger
Mark Pechenik

Photo Stylist
JoAnn Masaoka Van Atta

Photographers: Tom Wyatt (all except page 46); Jack McDowell (page 46).

Cover: Oak bullnosed stair treads and 1½-inch solid oak team up in this elegant bookcase. Penetrating oil and wax add the finishing touches. Photograph by Tom Wyatt. Design by Roger Flanagan.

Editor, Sunset Books:
Elizabeth L. Hogan

Third printing September 1989

Storage Solutions

For most of us, there's just never enough shelf or cabinet space. But this book can help you remedy the situation—it sets out in step-by-step instructions everything you'll need to know to design and build your own storage units.

We begin with a detailed look at the materials you'll need. Next, we survey basic woodworking tools and techniques—from measuring and marking lumber to sanding and finishing your completed project. In the third chapter, we show you the details of designing and building open shelves, bookcases, and cabinets. And if you're looking for specific ideas, you'll find a 20-page collection of distinctive storage projects you can tailor to your own situation.

We wish to acknowledge the American Plywood Association and the Hardwood Plywood Manufacturers Association for sharing with us information on their products. We are also grateful to Western Audio Imports for supplying props used in some of our photos.

Finally, we extend special thanks to Fran Feldman for editing the manuscript, and to Kathy Oetinger for cutting the screens for the illustrations.

CONTENTS

BASIC
MATERIALS

The materials you use for your bookshelf or cabinet are just as important to the appearance of the finished project as the workmanship that goes into it.

The basic materials—lumber, sheet products, and fasteners—are all discussed in this chapter. Once you're familiar with what's available in each category, you'll be better equipped to determine what it is you'll need.

Where can you find a good selection of materials? Try your local lumberyard or home improvement center first. For hard-to-find items such as hardwood plywoods, check the Yellow Pages. You'll find lumberyards that specialize in sheet products under "Plywoods and Veneers" and retailers who carry hardwoods under "Hardwoods." To chase down specialized nails, screws, or bolts, look under the specific fastener.

Of course, your project may require some additional hardware, such as shelf brackets, door hinges, or masonry fasteners. For information on these items, turn to the "Design & Assembly" chapter on pages 44–73.

Choosing Lumber

Wood is, of course, the starting point for any woodworking project. But for the uninitiated, dealing with the huge array of sizes, species, and grades of lumber can be overwhelming at first.

You may also be surprised at how crusty a busy lumberyard employee can be if you have no idea what you're looking for. On the other hand, armed with an understanding of some basic terms, you can usually secure friendly help with the fine points.

Lumberyard Lingo

For starters, you'll need to know the different types of lumber and how lumber is sold and sized.

Softwood or hardwood? Lumber is divided into softwoods and hardwoods, terms that refer to the origin of the wood. Softwoods come from conifers, hardwoods from deciduous trees. The terms can be misleading, however. Though hardwoods are usually harder than softwoods, some softwoods—like Douglas fir and southern pine—are actually harder than such so-called hardwoods as poplar, aspen, and Philippine mahogany (lauan).

As a rule, softwoods are less expensive, easier to tool, and more readily available than hardwoods. But the durable hardwoods have greater richness and diversity of color, grain, and texture than softwood.

For a closer look at the characteristics of individual softwoods and hardwoods, refer to the charts on pages 94–95.

How lumber is sold. Lumber may be sold by the lineal foot, the board foot, or even by the pound.

The *lineal foot* considers only the length of the piece. For example, you might ask for five 1 by 10s, each 8 feet long, or, put another way, 40 lineal feet of 1 by 10.

The *board foot* is the most common unit for volume orders; lumberyards often quote prices per 1,000 board feet. To compute board feet, use this formula: thickness in *inches* x width in *feet* x length in *feet*. For example, a 1 by 6 board 10 feet long would be computed as follows: 1″ x ½′(6″) x 10′ = 5 board feet.

The *pound* measure is sometimes used for fine hardwoods that are very dense or expensive.

Nominal and surfaced (actual) sizes. The beginner's most common stumbling block is assuming that a 2 by 4 board is actually 2 inches thick and 4 inches wide. It's not. Such numbers give the nominal size of the lumber—its size when sliced from the log. But when the piece is dried and surfaced (planed), it's reduced to a smaller size.

Almost all softwood lumber is surfaced on four sides (designated S4S), but some species are also sold rough—or unsurfaced—for outdoor use. Rough wood remains close to its nominal dimensions, but actual dimensions vary. The chart below lists the nominal sizes of softwood lumber and the standard surfaced dimensions for each size. The lumber is sold in lengths ranging from 6 to 20 feet in increments of 2 feet.

Standard Dimensions of Softwoods

Nominal size	Surfaced (actual) size
1 by 1	¾″ by ¾″
1 by 2	¾″ by 1½″
1 by 3	¾″ by 2½″
1 by 4	¾″ by 3½″
1 by 6	¾″ by 5½″
1 by 8	¾″ by 7¼″
1 by 10	¾″ by 9¼″
1 by 12	¾″ by 11¼″
2 by 2	1½″ by 1½″
2 by 3	1½″ by 2½″
2 by 4	1½″ by 3½″
2 by 6	1½″ by 5½″
2 by 8	1½″ by 7¼″
2 by 10	1½″ by 9¼″
2 by 12	1½″ by 11¼″
4 by 4	3½″ by 3½″

Buying hardwoods can be tricky, because they come in random widths and lengths, seemingly odd thicknesses, and often with rough edges.

You may see the term *four-quarter* or 4/4; like 1-by or 2-by, this represents the nominal thickness of a board. A rough 4/4 board is about 1 inch thick, a 5/4 board about 1¼ inches thick, an 8/4 board around 2 inches thick, and so on. Hardwoods are normally surfaced somewhat thicker than softwoods; for example, a 1-by is typically 13/16 inch thick instead of ¾ inch.

You may also find lumber designated S1S, S2S, S3S, and S4S, which mean surfaced one side, two sides, and so on. Hardwoods are often sold S2S, with the two wide faces having been planed. Surfaced boards found at retail outlets often have one or two straight edges as well. They may bear the stamp S/L1E, straight-line ripped on one edge, or S/L2E, straight-line ripped on two edges. This makes the board easier to cut to length or width with a table or radial-arm saw.

Unless you have a planer, you may need to have the lumberyard mill your hardwood lumber to the exact thickness. For minor resawing jobs, a table or band saw is usually sufficient.

Lumber Grading Guidelines

Lumber of the same species and size is graded on a scale: the top grade may be virtually flawless, the bottom grades virtually unusable.

All grading distinctions are based on defects. Decide what you can live with and buy the lowest acceptable grade. If you want a natural finish, buy top-grade lumber. If you plan to paint, buy a lower grade—paint can hide defects.

Softwood grades. Softwoods are broken down into two basic categories: dimension lumber (graded for strength) and boards (graded for appearance).

For bookshelves and cabinets, you'll usually need appearance-graded boards. The two main grades are Select

Choosing Lumber

(sometimes called clear) and Common, with several subgrades within each of these categories. Look for C-and-better Selects if you want flawless, knotless wood. Other popular choices for shelving are No. 2 and No. 3 Common "knotty" pine. Common boards marked Construction or Standard-and-better may be fine for utility shelves. Whatever the grade, let your eye be the final judge.

To thicken the plot, certain lumber species, notably redwood and Idaho white pine, have their own grading systems. Look for these grades of redwood, listed in descending order of quality: Clear All Heart, Clear, B grade, Select Heart, Select, Construction Heart, Construction Common, Merchantable Heart, and Merchantable. For Idaho white pine, the categories are Supreme, Choice, Quality, Sterling, Standard, and Utility.

Dimension lumber is rated primarily for strength in house framing, but it can be used in woodworking where extra strength or thickness is required. Select Structural is the top of the line.

Hardwood grades. Hardwoods are graded by the number of defects in a given length and width of board. The best grades are Firsts, Seconds, and a mix of the two called FAS. These grades apply to clear wood at least 8 feet long and 6 inches wide.

Next comes Select, which permits defects on the back. Select is followed by No. 1 and No. 2 Common. Lesser grades are often unusable.

Between FAS and Select are two subgrades: FAS 1 face and Select-and-better. The former, graded FAS on one side but No. 1 Common on the back, may be an economical choice if only one side will be visible.

Beyond Grading: How to Pick Lumber

Even within the same stack of lumber, you'll often find striking differences between individual pieces. Whenever possible, sort through the stacks yourself; most lumberyards will let you look and choose if you neatly repile the stacks. Here's what to look for.

Moisture content. When wood is sawn, it's still "green"—that is, unseasoned. Before it's ready for use, the best lumber is dried, either by air-drying or kiln-drying.

For interior woodworking projects, buy kiln-dried lumber whenever possible. If you do choose the air-dried type, look for wood stamped MC-15; this indicates a moisture content not exceeding 15 percent. If you opt for green wood, you're asking for trouble later, since the wood may split, warp, or shrink.

Vertical or flat grain? Depending on the cut of the millsaw, lumber will have either parallel grain lines running the length of the piece (vertical grain) or a marbled appearance (flat grain).

Vertical-grain lumber is stronger and less likely to warp or shrink noticeably. On the other hand, flat-sawing some-

times produces attractive "figure"—the patterns produced by knots, crotches, pores, and growth rings.

Heartwood or sapwood? The inactive wood nearest the center of a living tree is called heartwood. Sapwood, next to the bark, contains the growth cells. The main differences are color and density—heartwood is usually darker, denser, and more resistant to decay than sapwood.

Weathering and milling defects. Examine the available lumber closely for defects, many of which are illustrated below.

To test for warping, lift each piece at one end and sight down the face and edges. A *crook* (or crown) is an edgeline warp, a *bow* a face warp. *Cups* are bends across the face; *twists* are multiple bends. Pieces with long, gentle bends can sometimes be planed flat or made straight when they're nailed.

Other defects to look for include checks, splits, shakes, and wane. *Checks* are cracks along the annual growth rings in the wood, *splits* are checks that go all the way through the piece, and *shakes* are hollows between growth rings. *Wane* means that the edge or corner of the piece has either untrimmed bark or a lack of wood.

Also be on the lookout for such general problems as rotting, staining, insect holes, and pitch pockets (sap reservoirs below the surface). Try to avoid the bull's-eye pieces milled from the center of the log; they tend to crack and warp more easily than other pieces.

Common Lumber Defects

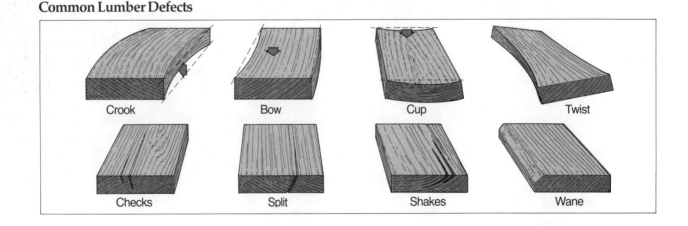

Crook   Bow   Cup   Twist

Checks   Split   Shakes   Wane

SNUG BY THE FIRE

Fitting snugly against this rustic stone fireplace, built-in solid oak cabinets with glass-paneled doors and commodious drawers blend smoothly with the adjacent oak mantelpiece and flooring. As shown at left, the decorative recessed panels at the top of the cabinets are trimmed with mahogany molding that richly enhances the oak's golden warmth. Design: Richard White.

Plywood, hardboard, and particleboard, all manufactured products, offer two main advantages over solid lumber: availability in large sheets and economy. Woodworking uses for sheet products include cabinetry, shelving, and countertops.

Plywood is probably the most familiar of the sheet products. But increasing in popularity are other sheet materials—hardboard, particleboard, and such new offshoots as fiberboard, waferboard, oriented strand board, and flakeboard.

PLYWOOD

Plywood is manufactured from thin wood veneers peeled from the log with a very sharp cutter and then glued together. The grain of each veneer runs perpendicular to the layers just above and below, making plywood strong in all directions.

Standard plywood size is 4 feet by 8 feet, though you can find—or special-order—plywood sheets that are 10 feet long.

The differences between an exterior and an interior grade of plywood are the type of glue used to make each one and the quality of the veneers. Exterior grades require weatherproof glue and higher-grade veneers. Use exterior grades for outdoor projects. For most other work, however, an interior grade of plywood (often labeled Exposure 1 or 2) will work perfectly well.

Like solid lumber, plywoods are divided into softwoods and hardwoods according to their face and back veneers only.

Softwood plywood. Though softwood plywood may be manufactured from any of 70 different species of wood, the most common by far are Douglas fir and southern pine. Species are rated for stiffness and strength, and placed in one of five groups, Group 1 being the strongest. The group number, along with other characteristics discussed in this section, appears on the stamp imprinted on the back or edge of each panel.

Panels are also rated by grade, determined by the appearance of the panel's face and back. The letters N and A through D designate the different grades (see chart below). Use top-of-the-line N grade where you want a perfect, natural finish; this grade may have to be special-ordered. Generally, presanded A and B grades are the choices where wood will be visible; lower grades are unsuitable for a fine finish.

Plywood comes in many face/back grade combinations, though your lumberyard may stock only a few. If both sides will be exposed, you'll probably want to choose A/B panels. A/C (exterior) or A/D (interior) panels are economical choices where only one side will be visible.

The most common thicknesses of standard softwood plywood range from ¼ to ¾ inch in ⅛-inch increments.

Hardwood plywood. Though more expensive than softwood types, hardwood plywood is often an economical alternative to solid hardwood. Hardwood plywood is identified by the veneer used on the face side of the panel. Popular domestic faces include ash, birch, black walnut, cherry, mahogany, maple, and oak. A number of imported woods are also available. Standard panel size is 4 by 8 feet; common thicknesses are ⅛ inch, ¼ inch, ½ inch, and ¾ inch.

Hardwood plywood grading has its own terms. The top of the line, A grade (sometimes called Premium), has well-matched veneers and uniform color, making it the best choice for a natural finish. Next comes B grade (Good or Number 1), which allows less well matched veneers and pinhole knots, and normally looks best when stained. Sound grade (Number 2), which still allows no open defects, is best painted. Face grades lower than Sound are generally not worth using.

You may also see the terms A2 and A3. Hardwood plywood that's graded A2 has the best grade veneer (either Premium or Good) on the face and Sound veneer on the back; the face and back veneers are usually the same species. Hardwood plywood graded A3 has a top-grade veneer on the face and Industrial (or Utility) veneer on the back; in this case, the back veneer may not be the same species as the face.

One of the most popular faces for hardwood plywood is birch; it's durable and attractive, tools cleanly, and is

The Softwood Plywood Grading System

Grade	Characteristics
N	Smooth-surface, "natural finish" veneer. Select, all heartwood, or all sapwood. Free of open defects. Allows no more than 6 repairs, wood only, for each 4 by 8 panel, made parallel to grain and well matched for grain and color.
A	Smooth; accepts paint. Allows no more than 18 neatly made repairs—boat, sled, or router type, and parallel to grain. May be used for natural finish in less demanding applications.
B	Solid surface; allows shims, circular repair plugs, and tight knots to 1 inch across grain. Some minor splits permitted.
C-Plugged	Improved C veneer. Allows splits no more than ⅛ inch wide, and knotholes and insect holes no more than ¼ by ½ inch. Some broken grain and synthetic repairs permitted.
C	Allows tight knots to 1½ inches, knotholes to 1 inch across grain and some to 1½ inches, if total width of knots and knotholes is within specified limits. Synthetic or wood repairs permitted, as are discolorations and sanding defects that don't impair strength. Limited splits and stitching permitted.
D	Allows knots and knotholes up to 2½ inches wide across grain and ½ inch larger within specified limits. Limited splits and stitching permitted. Available only in interior (Exposure 1 or 2) panels.

Chart courtesy of American Plywood Association

The Hardwood Plywood Grading System

Grade	Characteristics
A grade	Face smooth, tight-cut, and free of obvious defects. If face consists of more than one veneer, veneers must be carefully edge-matched by either book-matching or slip-matching (see illustration below).
B grade	Face smooth and tight-cut. If face consists of more than one veneer, sharp contrasts in grain, figure, and natural character markings are not permitted. May contain small burls or pinhole knots.
Sound (2)	Face free of open defects, but veneers not matched for grain or color. Knots to ¾ inch permitted; discoloration, rough areas, and patches allowed.
Industrial (3)	Allows knots and knotholes up to 1 inch, open splits up to ³/₁₆ inch, and crossbreaks and shakes 1 inch long. Veneers may overlap.
Specialty (SP)	Made to order. Includes decorative species such as wormy chestnut, bird's-eye maple, and English brown oak. (Veneers for wall paneling usually fall in this category.)

Chart based on material provided by Hardwood Plywood Manufacturers Association

one of the lowest-priced hardwood plywoods. You can increase your savings by choosing "shop" birch plywood—panels with slight defects that you can cut around.

One-piece, rotary-cut face veneers (see drawing below) have wavy, uninteresting grain; matched plain-sliced veneers are usually more attractive.

Some grades of plywood may have voids in the inner veneers, and these can be unsightly if the edges are to be exposed. Where appearance counts, you can putty the edges or cover them with wood tape or molding. Another solution is to buy lumber-core sheets. Made of face veneers glued to a solid lumber core, this plywood has easily worked edges and holds fasteners better than veneer-core plywood.

If you're planning to clear-finish the edges or you're simply looking for extra strength in thin sheets, opt for Baltic or Finnish plywood—birch panels made up of many very thin, solid veneers. They're available in sheets that measure 5 by 5 or 8 by 4 feet (the grain runs across the width).

HARDBOARD

Hardboard is produced by reducing waste wood chips to fibers and then bonding the fibers back together under pressure with natural or synthetic adhesives.

Harder, denser, and cheaper than plywood, hardboard is commonly manufactured in 4- by 8-foot sheets. It may be smooth on both sides or have a meshlike texture on the back. The two main types are standard and tempered. Standard hardboard can be painted easily; tempered hardboard, designed for strength and moisture resistance, is difficult to paint.

You'll usually see hardboard only in ⅛- and ¼-inch thicknesses. A similar but less dense product, fiberboard, is available in thicker sheets but is relatively difficult to find.

In woodworking, the main uses of standard, unfinished hardboard include bookcase and cabinet backs, sliding doors, and drawer bottoms. Perforated hardboard, sometimes called pegboard, is often combined with hooks, brackets, and racks for hanging storage.

Though relatively easy to cut and shape, hardboard dulls standard tools rapidly. If you plan to work much with hardboard, arm yourself with carbide-tipped saw blades. Hardboard also doesn't hold fasteners well; it's usually necessary to drive them through it into solid wood.

PARTICLEBOARD

Manufactured from chips and particles of waste wood, particleboard has a speckled appearance, in contrast to the smooth look of hardboard. Standard sheet size is 4 by 8 feet; common thicknesses range from ¼ to ¾ inch in ⅛-inch increments. Typical uses are for cabinet interiors, shelving, and core stock for plastic laminate countertops.

Several types of particleboard, marketed under different names, are available; some are designed for exterior use. Most common is a single-layer sheet with uniform density and particle size. But whenever possible, choose the triple-layer type with a denser, smoother face and back.

One drawback to particleboard is its weight. If you're using it for shelves, you'll need to support it at close intervals. And don't finish particleboard with a water-base paint; the water tends to soak in, causing the wood to swell.

You can work particleboard with standard cutting tools, but equip yourself with carbide-tipped saw blades and router bits. Because the urea-formaldehyde glues used to bond standard sheets are potentially toxic, wear a painter's mask while you work.

Particleboard won't hold fasteners well. For maximum strength, nail or screw through it into solid wood; if that's not possible, use nails and glue.

A Closer Look at Plywood

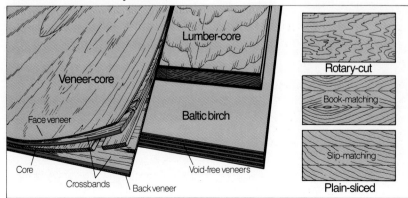

Veneer-core — Face veneer — Core — Crossbands — Back veneer

Lumber-core — Baltic birch — Void-free veneers

Rotary-cut — Book-matching — Slip-matching — Plain-sliced

CUSTOM-CUT CORNER

Echoing the same molding and style as the window trim, these split-level bookcases look right at home in this bright corner. Made from solid lumber, these traditional cases feature custom-shaped woodwork at the top and around the kickbase. As shown at right, a 1 by 1 strip fits snugly in matching notches to support each adjustable shelf. Design: Ruth Soforenko Associates.

FASTENERS

Nails, screws, bolts, and adhesives—these are the materials you'll need, either separately or in combination, to assemble any woodworking project.

Since the fastest way to join two pieces is to nail them together, nails are the most popular fastener for many jobs. When the project demands extra strength and a fine appearance, woodworkers usually use screws or an adhesive, or both. If strength alone is the issue, turn to oversize lag screws or bolts.

NAILS

Nails are sold in 1-, 5-, and 50-pound boxes, or loose in bins. Many different types are available. Here's a guide to the most commonly used nails. They're illustrated in the drawing below, at left.

The basic nail collection. For most uses, woodworkers will choose either box nails or finishing nails. Box nails come in sizes from 2-penny to 40-penny, finishing nails from 2-penny to 20-penny. *Penny* (abbreviated as d) once referred to the cost of 100 hand-forged nails; 3-penny nails, for instance, were 3 cents per hundred. The term now is used to indicate the length of a nail. The chart below illustrates the equivalents in inches of the most common nail sizes.

Other nails you'll want to have on hand include common nails and brads. Cement-coated nails are extra insurance against nail pullout. For outdoor projects, look for hot-dipped galvanized box, finishing, or common nails.

■ *Box nails.* Box nails have wide, flat heads to spread the load and resist pull-through. Though they're less likely to split wood than common nails, box nails bend much more easily when mis-hit.

■ *Finishing nails.* When you don't want the head of the nail to show, use a finishing nail. After driving it nearly flush, you sink the slightly rounded head with a nailset (see page 34).

■ *Common nails.* Similar in shape to box nails, common nails have an extra-thick shank. They're favored for heavy construction.

■ *Brads.* Resembling miniature finishing nails, brads are useful for joining thin pieces and for nailing into delicate ends or edges. Brads are sized by length and wire gauge; the higher the gauge, the thinner the brad.

SCREWS

Though more time-consuming to drive than nails, screws make stronger and neater joints, especially when combined with glue. Used without glue, screws can be removed so you can easily dismantle a joint.

Screw types. The array of different screws available to the woodworker can be bewildering. Discussed on the following page are the five types most commonly used in wood. They include three kinds of woodscrews, as well as

Types of Nails

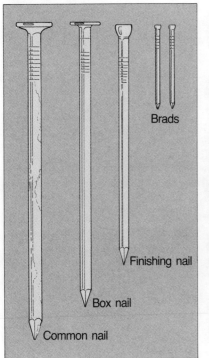

Brads

Finishing nail

Box nail

Common nail

Standard Nail Sizes

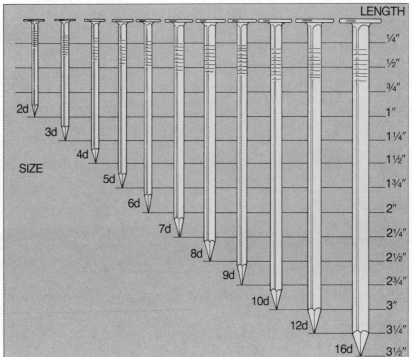

LENGTH

1/4"
1/2"
3/4"
1"
1 1/4"
1 1/2"
1 3/4"
2"
2 1/4"
2 1/2"
2 3/4"
3"
3 1/4"
3 1/2"

2d
3d
4d
SIZE
5d
6d
7d
8d
9d
10d
12d
16d

FASTENERS

drywall screws and lag screws (see drawing below). If you need to screw into metal, try a sixth screw type, the self-tapping sheet metal screw.

■ *Flathead screws.* The most common screw, the slotted steel flathead sits flush with the material's surface. For a decorative touch, you can use brass flathead screws with finishing washers.

The only difference between the Phillips head and the slotted flathead screw is the cross pattern notched in the head, which keeps the screwdriver from slipping.

■ *Ovalhead screws.* These partially recessed screws are used for attaching exposed hardware.

■ *Roundhead screws.* Roundheads, which sit atop the wood, are used to hold thin materials between the screw head and the surface.

■ *Drywall screws.* Bugle-head drywall screws, originally designed for fastening gypsum wallboard to wall studs and ceiling joists, are becoming popular with woodworkers. These versatile fasteners, now widely available as "multipurpose" screws, are a big improvement over traditional woodscrews: they're sharper and better machined, and the Phillips heads won't strip as easily. You'll know them by their flat black finish.

■ *Lag screws.* These heavy-duty fasteners are oversize screws with square or hexagonal heads. Use them with a flat washer and drive them with a wrench or ratchet and socket (see page 39).

Screw sizes. Woodscrews are sized both by length (from ¼ to 4 inches) and, for thickness, by wire gauge number (0 to 24—about ¹⁄₁₆ to ⅜ inch). In general, the higher the gauge number for a given length of screw, the greater its holding ability.

The chart below shows the most common screw gauges and the lengths available for each one. Gauge numbers 0 and 1 are available only in ¼-inch lengths. Few hardware stores stock screws smaller than number 2 or larger than number 14.

Drywall screws are readily available in lengths ranging from ¾ inch to 3 inches. For screws up to 2 inches in length, gauge number is normally fixed at 6; longer screws are typically number 8.

Lag screws have ¼- to ½-inch-diameter shafts; lengths range from 1 to 12 inches.

BOLTS

Unlike the screw's tapered point, which digs into wood, a bolt's straight, threaded shaft passes completely through the materials being joined; the bolt is fastened down with a nut screwed onto its end. Bolts are stronger fasteners than nails or screws because the material is gripped from both sides.

Types of bolts. Most bolts are made from zinc-coated steel, but brass bolts are also available. The machine bolt's hexagonal head is driven with a wrench. Carriage bolts have self-

Types of Screws

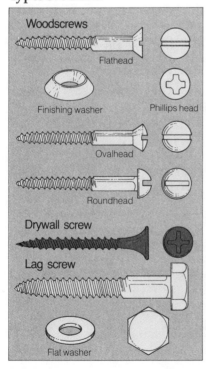

Common Woodscrew Sizes

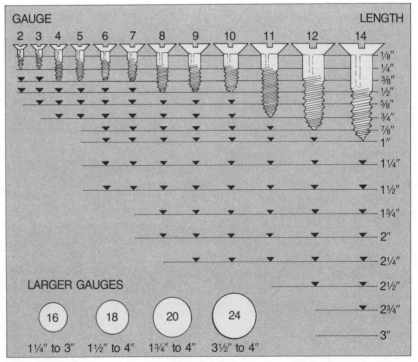

Shortest lengths in gauges 2 to 14 are shown actual size; other lengths are indicated by arrow points.

anchoring heads that dig into the wood as you tighten the nut. Stove bolts are slotted for screwdrivers. All three types are shown at right.

Bolt sizes. Bolts are classified by their diameter (⅛ to 1 inch) and length (⅜ inch and up). If you can't find a bolt that's long enough for your job, use a threaded rod (a headless bolt shaft) cut to length with a hacksaw; then add a nut and washer at each end of the threaded rod.

Nuts and washers. Hexagonal nuts are the standard, but you'll also see square nuts, wingnuts, nylon-insert locknuts, T-nuts, and acorn nuts. Wingnuts can be quickly tightened or loosened by hand. Nylon-insert locknuts hold the bolt tightly in place without marring the wood. T-nuts are driven flush into the bottom material, preventing them from rotating. Where appearance counts, use acorn nuts.

Most bolts need a flat, round washer at each end. Self-anchoring bolts, such as carriage bolts, require only one washer, inside the nut. Lock washers help keep nuts from working loose.

Bolts, Nuts & Washers

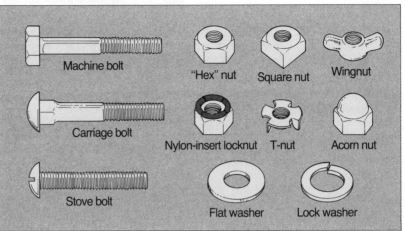

ADHESIVES

When used correctly, a good adhesive creates a neat, permanent joint that's as strong as—or stronger than—the wood itself.

Adhesives vary according to strength, water resistance, ability to fill gaps, and setting time. For general work, most woodworkers reach for white (PVA) or yellow (aliphatic resin) glue. For outdoor use, waterproof resorcinol is the standard.

Other adhesives meet specialized needs: epoxy bonds unlike materials; contact cement secures plastic laminate; hide glue has a long setting time; and instant glue positions awkward-shaped pieces that can't be clamped.

The chart below will acquaint you with the pros and cons of all these adhesives.

Woodworking Adhesives

Type	Characteristics	Uses
White (common household) glue (polyvinyl acetate)	Rigid bond. Difficult to sand (clogs sandpaper); softens above 150°F. Not waterproof.	Good for indoor use where heat and moisture are not factors (must be clamped).
Yellow (carpenter's or wood) glue (aliphatic resin)	Rigid bond. Dries clear and can be sanded; heat-resistant. Can be applied at temperatures as low as 50°F; not waterproof.	Best glue for general woodworking (more moisture-resistant than white glue); good for indoor use and large assemblies (must be clamped). Fills gaps between materials.
Resorcinol glue (marine resin)	Strong, rigid, permanent bond. Must be mixed; can be sanded. Waterproof; dries dark. Toxic (releases formaldehyde).	Bonds wood in high-moisture applications (must be clamped); fills gaps between materials.
Epoxy resin	Strong, rigid, permanent bond. Must be mixed; waterproof. Uncured epoxy is toxic.	Good for outdoor projects, repairs, and joints that can't be clamped; bonds unlike materials. Fills gaps between materials (choose type formulated to work with wood; don't buy quick-setting type).
Contact cement	Bonds on contact; water-resistant.	Bonds thin materials to a base; use to attach plastic laminate to wood (choose newer, water-base types, if available).
Liquid hide glue	Strong bond. Slow to set; can be sanded. Not waterproof. Reversible.	Good for complicated assemblies (must be tightly clamped).
Instant glue (cyanoacrylate)	Instant, strong bond; water-resistant.	Secures materials that can't be clamped; use to bond nonporous materials to wood (won't set instantly if wood is acidic). CAUTION: Bonds quickly to skin.

FINISHING PRODUCTS

A good finish keeps dirt and moisture out of wood pores, wards off dents and scratches, and enhances the appearance of fine wood.

The chart below sets out the basics. It's divided into stains, penetrating finishes, and finishes that sit on the surface of the wood.

Stains aren't final finishes. They're used for coloring wood to make it look aged or similar to another wood. You'll still need to apply a protective finish on top.

For a "bare wood" look, you'll generally want to turn to a penetrating finish. Use a surface finish for more complete protection and a glassier appearance. A coat of wax adds depth and luster to any finish.

If you're in doubt about what finish to choose, ask your paint dealer. Comparing notes with other woodworkers is also an excellent way of finding a reliable finish.

Stains

Pigmented oil stain	Simple to apply; won't fade or bleed. Useful for making one wood species look like another. Heavy pigments tend to obscure grain and gum up pores in hardwoods such as oak and walnut. Not compatible with shellac or lacquer.
Penetrating oil stain	Stains with dyes rather than pigments, so pores and grain are revealed. Similar to penetrating resin, but with color added. Produces irregular results on softwoods and plywoods.
Water stain	Colors are brilliant, clear, and permanent. Since water raises wood grain, resanding is necessary. Very slow drying. Sold in powdered form.
Non-grain-raising stain	Bright, transparent colors; won't raise wood grain. Available premixed by mail. Very short drying time; best when sprayed. Not for use on softwoods.

Penetrating Finishes

Boiled linseed oil	Lends warm, slightly dull patina to wood. Dries very slowly and requires many coats. Moderate resistance to heat, water, and chemicals. Easily renewable.
Tung oil	Natural oil finish that's hard and highly resistant to abrasion, moisture, heat, acid, and mildew. Requires several thin, hand-rubbed applications (heavy coats wrinkle badly). Best with polymer resins added.
Penetrating resin (Danish oil, antique oil)	Use on hard, open-grain woods. Leaves wood looking and feeling "natural." Easy to apply and retouch, but doesn't protect against heat or abrasion. May darken some woods.
Rub-on varnish	Penetrating resin and varnish combination that builds up sheen as coats are applied; dries fairly quickly. Moderately resistant to water and alcohol; darkens wood.

Surface Finishes

Shellac	Lends warm luster to wood. Easy to apply, retouch, and remove. Excellent sealer. Lays down in thin, quick-drying coats that can be rubbed to a very high sheen. Little resistance to heat, alcohol, and moisture.
Lacquer (nitrocellulose)	Strong, clear, quick-drying finish in both spraying and brushing form; very durable, though vulnerable to moisture. Requires 3 or more coats; can be polished to a high gloss.
Alkyd varnish	Widely compatible oil-base interior varnish that produces a thick coating with good overall resistance. Dries slowly and darkens with time. Brush marks and dust can be a problem.
Phenolic-resin varnish (spar varnish)	Tough, exterior varnish with excellent weathering resistance; flexes with wood's seasonal changes. To avoid yellowing, product should contain ultraviolet absorbers.
Polyurethane varnish	Thick, plastic, irreversible coating that's nearly impervious to water, heat, and alcohol. Dries overnight. Incompatible with some stains and sealers. Follow instructions to ensure good bonding between coats.
Water-base varnish	Water base makes for easy cleanup, but raises wood grain. Not as heat- or water-resistant as alkyd varnish, nor as chemical-resistant as polyurethane.
Enamel	Available in flat, semigloss, and gloss finishes and in a wide range of colors. May have lacquer or varnish (alkyd, polyurethane, or acrylic) base; each shares same qualities as clear finish of the same type.
Wax	Occasionally used as a finish, but more often applied over harder top coats. Increases luster of wood. Not very durable, but offers some protection against liquids when renewed frequently.

WARMTH OF WALNUT

A built-in wall system of traditional elegance warms up this room with the luster of black walnut. Decorative molding on both the shelves and raised-bevel door panels adds character. For ease of construction, the components of this unit were built separately, then assembled in place. Wide molding conceals the gap near the ceiling. Architect: Bob Fleury.

TOOLS
&
TECHNIQUES

To build any woodworking project, certain steps are essential—you'll have to measure, cut, shape, drill, fasten, and finish. On the following pages, we'll introduce you to the basic tools and techniques required for each step.

Do you need expensive power tools to build bookshelves and cabinets? Not really. The bare necessities—a rule, saw, drill, and hammer—will see you through many projects. However, sophisticated casework may require very accurate cuts and joinery, and that's where power tools are helpful. The choice is yours—we've included instructions for using both hand and power tools.

Remember that buying quality tools will save you money in the long run. To find them, look in hardware stores, woodworking specialty shops, or mail-order catalogs. You may also want to ask other woodworkers or a knowledgeable dealer for recommendations.

Measuring & Marking

The same modest beginnings—accurate measurement, layout, and marking—launch all successful woodworking projects. If you choose quality layout tools, work carefully, and remember the old rule "Measure twice, cut once," you'll be on your way to fine results.

Basic Layout Tools

Though hundreds of tools are available for measuring and marking, most shelving and cabinet projects require only a small collection. These are the basics.

Tape measure. For all-round utility, look for a 12- to 16-foot flexible tape, ¾ inch wide, marked with ¹⁄₁₆-inch graduations. Be sure the model you choose has a locking button to keep the tape from retracting. The end hook should be loosely riveted to adjust for precise inside and outside readings.

Combination square. The combination square allows you to lay out and check 90° and 45° angles, as well as perform other tasks. The tool's sliding handle can be tightened anywhere along the blade, or the blade can be removed and used as a bench rule. Many combination squares include a spirit level and a removable scribe for marking fine lines. Test a combination square carefully: many modestly priced models have play between the handle and blade.

Carpenter's square. When a combination square is too small, the 24- by 16-inch carpenter's square is ideal for laying out and checking square. The most durable squares—and the heaviest—are made from steel.

Adjustable T-bevel. The pivoting, locking blade on a T-bevel enables you to set the blade at any angle between 0° and 180°; to determine the correct setting, use a protractor or simply match an existing angle.

Scratch awl. Though the trusty pencil will see you through most marking tasks, a scratch awl will mark finer lines when precision really counts. Remember, though, that unlike a pencil line, these lines can't be erased.

Marking gauge. With this simple tool, you can accurately scribe width and thickness lines parallel to any straight edge. Some models include a graduated scale on the beam for quick reference.

Chalkline. A long, spool-wound cord housed inside a chalk-filled case, the chalkline is handy for dividing up sheet materials. Be sure your chalkline is equipped with an end hook.

Compass or dividers. Essential for drawing circles and arcs with radii of up to about 5 inches, a compass or dividers (the terms are often interchanged) can also be used to "step

Layout Tools

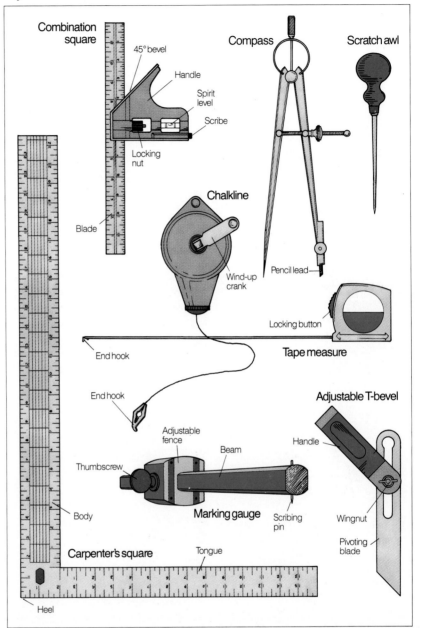

Combination square — 45° bevel, Handle, Spirit level, Scribe, Locking nut, Blade

Compass — Pencil lead

Scratch awl

Chalkline — Wind-up crank

Tape measure — Locking button, End hook

Carpenter's square — End hook, Thumbscrew, Body, Heel, Tongue

Marking gauge — Adjustable fence, Beam, Scribing pin

Adjustable T-bevel — Handle, Wingnut, Pivoting blade

WEDGED IN PLACE

Economizing space alongside the desk, this triangular-shaped bookcase allows maximum storage while doubling as a room divider between office and sitting areas. Like the desk, the bookcase is finished in easy-to-clean plastic laminate. The shelves adjust on metal pins that fit in holes drilled into the sides of the case. Design: Barbara Jacobs.

Measuring & Marking

off" equal measurements. Look for the type that allows you to replace one metal leg with a pencil lead.

Layout Tips

Whether you're marking cutoff lines on 1 by 10 shelves, dividing up ¾-inch plywood for cabinet components, or simply scribing a board for uniform width and thickness, you'll find tried-and-true techniques below.

Measuring tips. For accurate measurements, always follow the edge of the material with your tape measure and pull the end hook tightly against the board's end. Twist the tape slightly (see drawing at right) so the graduation is right down on the work. Mark the correct distance carefully with a straight line or draw a "crow's foot" (V-mark) that points right to the graduation.

Use existing pieces as patterns whenever possible. If you're copying another piece, use it to transfer dimensions directly.

Marking boards for length. To lay out the length of a board, start at one end, well beyond any visible defects in the wood, and square a line across the face. Then cut the board along this line. Measure the desired distance from the new end, mark the point, and draw a second line through this point.

When you draw a line, hold the square's handle firmly against the edge of the board and incline your pencil away from the straightedge at about a 60° angle, as shown at far right; angle scribing tools slightly, too.

Dividing up sheet products. Before beginning any layout work on plywood or another sheet product, check both the squareness and the dimensions of the piece. You may want to first do a rough layout with a chalkline, just to cut the sheet up into more manageable pieces. To use the chalkline, pull the chalk-covered cord from the case and stretch it taut between two points. Then lift it straight up near one end and release it quickly so it

snaps down sharply, leaving a long, straight line of chalk.

When marking for your finish cuts, a carpenter's square is handy: hold the square's tongue or body against the edge of the material and mark along the other side, as shown at bottom left. For longer cutting lines, mark both edges of the piece; then use a long straightedge to connect the points.

Whenever you're dividing up a sheet, be sure to account for the width of the kerf (cut) made by the blade you're going to use. It's simplest to lay out and cut the pieces one by one,

making each new cut on the waste side of the lines.

Scribing width and thickness. The simplest and most accurate way to lay out width and thickness dimensions is with a marking gauge.

To scribe a width line, set the gauge's adjustable fence to the correct distance, position the tool as shown at bottom right, and push the gauge away from you down the board's face. To lay out thickness, set the fence as required and push the gauge down the edge of the board.

Measuring & Marking Techniques

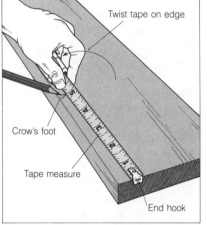

When using a steel tape, *pull the hook tight and twist the tape on edge. A crow's foot helps mark the graduation.*

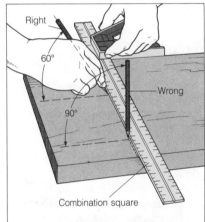

To draw a cutoff line, *hold the pencil at a 60° angle; keep the square's handle snug against the board's edge.*

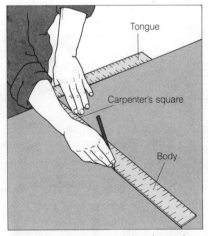

The carpenter's square *is best for marking plywood cuts. Place one side against the edge and draw along the other.*

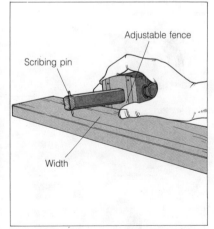

To scribe with a marking gauge, *set the fence, angle the scribing pin, and push the gauge away from you.*

CUTTING

Accurate, consistent cutting is essential to strong, square joints and assemblies. With that goal in mind, we present three levels of woodworking saws—handsaws, portable power saws, and stationary machines.

You could, if necessary, make most cuts with just a few handsaws. But by adding a portable circular saw and a saber saw to your collection, you'll make your work much easier.

Stationary machines—the table saw and radial-arm saw—are in a class by themselves in terms of both performance and price. Learn with the basic saws; then move up to a stationary machine as your needs and budget dictate.

HANDSAWS

A basic collection of handsaws would include a crosscut saw for cutting lumber and plywood to length, a ripsaw for cutting with the grain, and a back saw and a coping saw for joinery and curves. A compass saw is handy for rough cutouts.

A saw's function is a product of its shape, its blade size, and the position and number of teeth along the blade. The term *point* commonly applied to a saw's blade indicates both tooth size and number of teeth per inch (often

Crosscutting Techniques

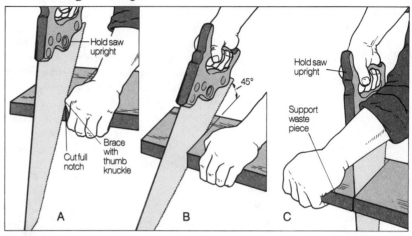

Crosscutting is easier *if you start with a full notch (A); once the cut is underway, lower the angle of the saw to 45° (B). At the end of a cut, support the waste piece with your free hand and finish with short, upright strokes (C).*

abbreviated as tpi). An 8-point saw has only 7 teeth per inch, since the points at both ends of that inch are included. In general, the fewer the teeth, the rougher and faster the cut; many teeth means a smooth but slower cut.

Cutting characteristics are also affected by the amount of *set*. Saw teeth are bent outward to produce a cut wider than the blade; without this set, the saw would bind in the cut, or *kerf*. Once more, the wider set produces a faster but rougher cut. The smaller the set, the finer the kerf.

Where saw teeth exit, wood will tend to splinter and break away. With any handsaw, cut with the good side of the wood *up,* or facing you.

Crosscut saw. Designed to cut across wood grain, the crosscut saw can also be used as an all-purpose saw on sheet products. Blade lengths vary from about 20 to 26 inches; the 26-inch length is a good first choice. For rough, fast cutting, an 8-point saw is most effective, but the slower 10-point model yields smoother results.

Basic Handsaws

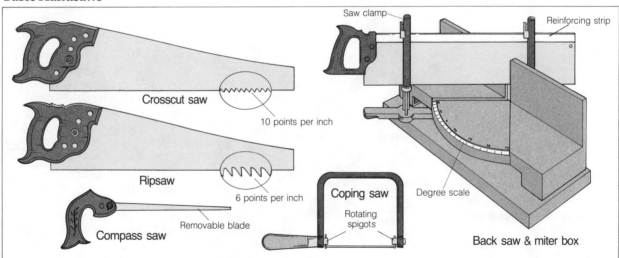

Crosscut saws do most of their cutting on the push stroke. Holding the saw nearly vertical, start the cut by slowly drawing the blade *up* a few times to make a notch; use the thumb of your free hand, as shown on the facing page, to guide the saw at first. A full notch cut about ½ inch into the far edge of the board will help guide the saw for the remainder of the cut.

Once the cut is underway, lower the saw's angle to about 45° (30° for plywood) and progress to smooth, full strokes. Align the saw by sighting down the back from above; keep your forearm and shoulder in line with the teeth. Be sure all the saw's kerf is on the waste side of your cutting line, or the finished piece will be too short. Woodworkers often cut a little wide of the line intentionally and dress the cut flush with a plane.

As you near the end of the cut, reach around the saw, as shown, and support the end of the waste piece. Return the saw to the vertical position and make the last strokes slowly and smoothly to avoid breaking off the waste piece and splintering the board.

Ripsaw. A specialized version of the crosscut saw, the ripsaw has larger, chisel-like teeth that cut rapidly in line with the wood grain. Ripsaws are available with 5, 5½, or 6 points per inch. If you're planning to buy a portable circular saw, skip the ripsaw—your crosscut saw will handle any occasional hand-ripping tasks.

Ripping—cutting in line with the wood grain—calls for techniques very similar to crosscutting. If you're using a ripsaw instead of a crosscut saw, hold the blade at a slightly steeper angle—about 60° (see at right). Again, you may wish to cut slightly wide of the line and dress the edge with a plane.

Unless you're making a short cut—3 feet or less—be sure to support both ends of the piece. If the saw binds, stick a nail in the cut behind the saw to spread it open.

Back saw. Designed for very fine, straight crosscuts in narrow stock, the rectangular-shaped back saw derives its name from a metal reinforcing strip that runs the length of the back and

Ripping a Long, Wide Board

To rip cleanly, *hold the ripsaw at a 60° angle, bracing the work with your knee and hand and supporting the board on two sawhorses. To cut around the sawhorses, simply move the board forward and back.*

Fine Cuts with Two Handsaws

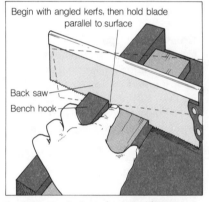

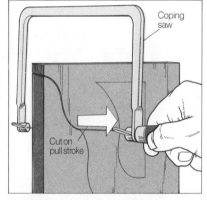

Back saw technique *begins with an angled kerf at each end. Then swing the saw parallel to the work and cut.*

A coping saw *cuts fine curves near an edge. For easier cutting, rotate the teeth and clear the waste as you go.*

prevents bowing. The typical back saw (sometimes called a tenon saw) has a 12- to 14-inch blade with 12 to 16 teeth per inch.

A *miter box* or bench hook is often used to guide the back saw into materials at a fixed 90° or 45° angle. Integral back saw / miter box units, with saws up to 30 inches in length, cut any angle from 45° to 90°; though more costly, these units are more precise.

Unlike the crosscut saw, the back saw is held so the blade is parallel to the cutting surface.

Coping saw. A thin, wiry blade strung taut within a small, rectangular frame enables the coping saw to make fine, accurate cuts and follow tight curves; cutting, however, is limited to

surfaces that its relatively shallow frame will fit around.

If you're cutting on a sawhorse, point the teeth away from the handle and cut on the push stroke. If the material is being held in a vise, point the teeth toward the handle and cut on the pull stroke. When cutting, the blade can be rotated to any position by turning the spigots holding the blade.

The coping saw also makes cutouts near an edge: detach the blade, slip it through a predrilled hole, and re-attach it.

Compass saw. No handsaw makes cutouts as easily as the compass saw. The thin blade, 10 to 14 inches long, tapers from about an inch at the handle to a point at the tip.

CUTTING

To begin a cutout, first drill a pilot hole in the waste area for the saw's blade. Once the cut is underway, it's best to switch to a crosscut saw for a long, straight cut.

PORTABLE CIRCULAR SAW

Using a circular saw and the correct blade, you can easily cut 10 times faster than with a crosscut saw. Common models range in size from 5½ to 8¼ inches (the size refers to the largest diameter of blade that the saw can accommodate). The popular 7¼-inch saw cuts through surfaced 2-by lumber at any angle from 45° to 90°.

Basic operation. For most cuts, you'll want the blade adjusted to 90°. Loosen the angle adjustment lock and push on the baseplate until it stops in the horizontal position; then retighten the lock. If you're cutting a bevel, set the blade with the help of the degree scale on the saw's body; then test the setting on scrap. For most materials, you'll want the blade to protrude only ¹⁄₁₆ to ⅛ inch below the cut.

Because the blade cuts upward, the material's top surface tends to splinter; place the best side *down*. To start a cut, rest the saw's baseplate on the stock and line up the blade with the waste side of your cutting line. Release the safety button, if the saw has one, and press the trigger. Let the motor reach speed; then slowly begin the cut. Depending on your saw type, you'll either aim the blade directly from the side or use the gunsight notch on the baseplate. (Gunsight notches are often inaccurate, so be sure to test yours before using it.)

If the saw binds, check that your support is adequate. On long rips, place a large nail in the kerf to prevent binding.

As you near the end, be sure you're in position to support the saw's weight. If necessary, grip the saw's front handle with your free hand. When you're crosscutting an unsupported piece, accelerate at the end to avoid splintering. Always let the blade stop completely before you swing the saw up or set it down.

Crosscutting tips. What's the secret to really straight cuts with this saw? You can clamp a straight length of scrap lumber to the material to guide the saw's baseplate, use a manufactured guide, or build a simple cutoff jig as shown below. Measure from the blade to the edge of the baseplate; clamp the guide at that distance from your cutting line.

Ripping. To guide a rip near a board's edge, use the ripping fence available for most saws. Set the blade at the minimum depth and attach the fence loosely. Line the blade up with the correct width marked at the board's end

Circular Saw

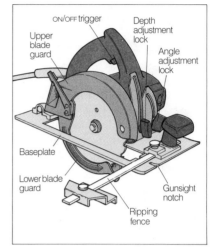

and tighten the fence. Be sure to account for the blade's kerf.

For wider rips, clamp a long scrap guide to the material or construct a ripping jig, as shown below.

Ripping can be slow, dusty work and is especially prone to kickback. Cut by pushing the saw slowly away from you. When you need to reposition yourself, back the saw off an inch or so in the kerf and let the blade stop while you move farther down the line.

SABER SAW

The saber saw's specialty is curves, circles, and cutouts, but you can also use it for straight cutting and beveling.

Crosscutting & Ripping with the Circular Saw

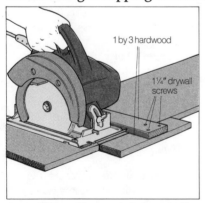

A cutoff jig *guides repeated crosscuts. Be sure the two hardwood strips are at an exact 90° angle to each other.*

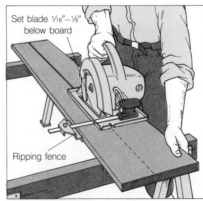

When ripping a board *to width, guide the cut with a ripping fence, holding the fence tightly against the edge.*

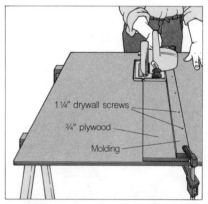

A ripping jig *directs a cut in a wide panel; make one from scrap plywood and a straight length of molding.*

CENTER OF ATTENTION

Chopping, mixing, cooking, and recipe-selecting take place with equal ease at this multipurpose kitchen island, which at once frees surrounding counters and puts floor space to good use. On the side, false door fronts flank a narrow cupboard between drawers. The drawer fronts are edged to match the frame of the frame-and-panel cabinet doors. Architect: Michael D. Moyer.

CUTTING

This saw's high-speed motor drives one of many interchangeable blades in an up-and-down (reciprocating) motion. Saber saws are available in single-speed, two-speed, and variable-speed models.

A variable-speed saw accelerates as you squeeze down on the trigger, allowing fine control when cutting tight curves or different materials. Look for a saw with a tilting baseplate for cutting bevels to 45°. An adjustable ripping fence and a circle guide (often the ripping fence turned upside down) are two useful accessories.

Since the saber saw's upward-cutting blade may cause the material's top surface to splinter, place the best side *down*. Be sure to wear safety goggles.

Curves and circles. When cutting tight curves, resist the urge to "steer" the saw by raising the baseplate—the angle of the cut will go askew. Instead, go as slowly as possible. If the curve is too tight, cut into the waste area to remove part of it; then return and finish the curve. If you're having a persistent problem keeping the blade on line, it's probably bent; replace the blade.

You can execute a circle with a radius of up to about 7 inches with the help of a circle guide.

Cutouts. To cut rectangular or curved cutouts inside a panel, it's simplest to

Saber Saw

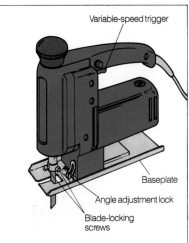

first drill a pilot hole in the waste area for the blade, as shown in the drawing below.

With practice, you can also start the cutout in thin materials by "plunge-cutting" with a rough-cutting blade. Rock the saw forward onto the baseplate's front edge, making sure the blade is free of the material. Turn on the saw; then slowly lower it until the blade tip cuts into the material and the baseplate rests flat on the surface.

Now cut the basic outline. If the corners must be square, round them off on the first pass; then finish them by sawing into the corners (see drawing below). For tightly curved corners, first drill the arcs with an electric

drill fitted with a brad point or multi-spur bit (see page 32).

TABLE SAW

The table saw is the cabinetmaker's standby for clean, straight cuts in both solid lumber and plywood. Table saws are sized by the maximum-diameter blade that will fit the saw. For all-round work, look for a 10-inch model equipped with at least a 1-horsepower motor.

The keys to a table saw's accuracy are an accurate rip fence and a miter gauge that slides in one of two carefully machined slots in the table surface. Blade height and tilt are controlled by cranks located below the table.

In addition to the features described above, your saw should include a clear safety guard over the blade and a splitter behind the blade to keep the stock from binding or kicking back.

When cutting, set the blade height ⅛ to ¼ inch above the stock and keep your hands as far away from the blade as you can. Leave the blade guard in place whenever possible. (We don't show the blade guard in our drawings for clarity only.) Place the good side of the stock *up* and be sure to wear safety goggles.

Crosscutting tips. The miter gauge guides crosscuts. Place it either in the left- or right-hand table slot (most woodworkers prefer the left). Set the

Curves & Cutouts with the Saber Saw

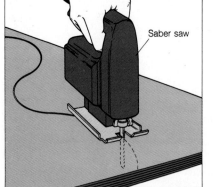

Cutting curves *is the saber saw's specialty. Cut tight curves slowly: a bent blade throws the cut's angle out of line.*

To make rectangular cutouts, *it's easiest to start from a pilot hole; cut the basic outline and then square each corner. To "plunge-cut" without a pilot hole (see inset), slowly lower the saw's baseplate onto the material.*

tilt scale for a 90° cut and check the blade angle with a square. Screw a hardwood auxiliary fence to the gauge for a safer, more accurate cut.

Hold the stock firmly against the gauge or auxiliary fence with your left hand, as shown, and push the gauge past the blade with your right hand. To cut wide material, reverse the gauge in the slot and push it through with the stock behind. A cutoff box (see page 56) is helpful for crosscutting large boards or sheet materials.

For repeated cuts of the same length, clamp a stop block to either the rip or auxiliary fence. Don't use the rip fence as a stop—the waste will bind and kick back. Provide support for long pieces: an extension table or a helper is a must to keep the pieces level.

Ripping. Ripping is the table saw's specialty, but it also requires the most care. The cut is guided by the rip fence, positioned either to the right or left of the blade (most woodworkers prefer the right). Line up the fence, measure the distance from blade tooth to fence (at both the front and back of the blade), and lock the fence securely. To provide support at the rear of the table when ripping long boards or sheet materials, you'll need a helper or an extension table.

Ripping is prone to kickback: stand to one side while you're working. Don't rip twisted, badly cupped, or narrow, knotted pieces.

Table Saw Details

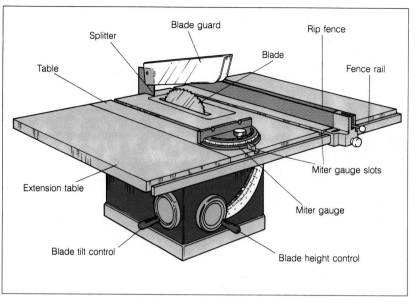

Hold the piece firmly against the rip fence with your left hand, as shown below, and feed the stock with your right hand. If you're ripping narrow stock, use a homemade push stick (shown below) as you near the end of the cut. This will help keep your hands a safe distance from the blade.

A *featherboard*, a 1 by 6 board mitered and kerfed at one end, provides both pressure and "give" when ripping. Using a clamp, attach the featherboard to the table in line with the front of the blade.

Mitering. Like crosscutting, mitering is guided by the miter gauge. Again, an auxiliary fence attached to the gauge improves the bearing surface. Check the angle; for best results, also make a test cut. To prevent the stock from "creeping" as it meets the blade, glue a strip of sandpaper to the auxiliary fence. If possible, keep the gauge angled in the direction shown.

Beveling. Beveling combines crosscutting, ripping, or mitering techniques with the correct blade tilt. Set

Three Table Saw Cuts

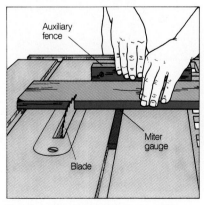

For clean crosscuts, *fasten an auxiliary fence to the miter gauge and push the stock and gauge past the blade.*

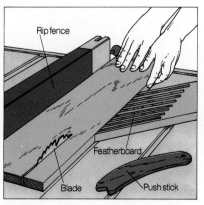

To rip a board, *set the rip fence and feed the stock as shown. Use a homemade push stick to finish a narrow rip.*

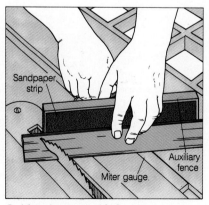

Guide miter cuts *with the miter gauge and auxiliary fence. Set the gauge angle; then cut slowly as if crosscutting.*

WOODCRAFTED ENCLOSURE

Defining an intimate dining area within a much larger living space, these handsome room dividers anchor to posts with wedge-shaped connecting blocks. Built from clear redwood milled from a wine vat and faced with oak plywood, the units look equally attractive from both sides. As shown at right, decorative birch plugs conceal the screws fastening the dadoed shelves to the uprights.

CUTTING

the blade angle with the help of the blade tilt control; then check it on a piece of scrap.

RADIAL-ARM SAW

The radial-arm saw has one advantage over the table saw: it crosscuts long boards handily. The main disadvantages are that it's awkward to rip—or even crosscut—wide sheet materials, and that the saw is very difficult to keep in fine adjustment.

Radial-arm saws are available in 9-, 10-, and 12-inch versions for the home workshop; a 10-inch saw with a 1½-horsepower motor is a good choice. Be sure the cutting capacity is up to your needs (your saw should be able to crosscut or rip 24 inches). For safety, your saw should include an adjustable blade guard and anti-kickback fingers, which help prevent kickback when you're ripping.

When using the radial-arm saw, always keep a 6-inch margin of safety between your hands and the blade, and be sure to wear safety goggles to protect your eyes.

Crosscutting tips. Begin by setting the blade for a 90° cut; set both the miter and bevel scales at 0°. With the elevating handle, position the blade about ⅛ inch below the table surface.

Radial-arm Saw Components

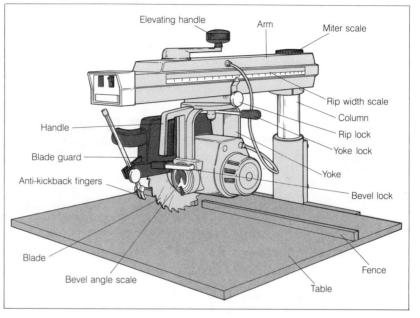

Loosen the rip lock so the motor is free to slide up and down the arm.

Place the stock—good side *up*— against the fence and hold it there with your free hand, as shown below. Squeeze the trigger, let the motor reach speed, and pull the blade smoothly through the stock. As soon as the blade completes the cut, push it back through the kerf and behind the fence.

If you have several boards to cut, "gang-cut" them all at once, as shown in the inset below. Extra-wide boards

and sheet materials can be crosscut as far as possible on the first pass and then turned end-for-end and finished with a second pass.

Mitering. Precise 45° miters can be tricky to cut and match by the standard method—rotating the arm. The solution? Build a simple miter jig, as shown below. After positioning the jig tightly against the fence, you simply use the crosscut position for either left- or right-hand miters.

Basic Crosscutting...

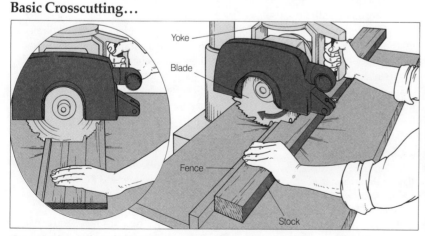

Crosscutting *is the radial-arm saw's specialty. Hold the stock tightly against the fence, draw the blade through, and then return the blade behind the fence. You can also "gang-cut" several pieces (see inset at left).*

...& Mitering

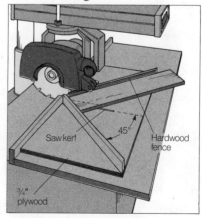

A miter jig *helps produce accurate cuts: simply position the jig against the fence and use the crosscut position.*

SHAPING TOOLS

After pieces have been sawn, they may require additional cutting, shaping, and smoothing before they can be assembled.

Chisels help pare notches and grooves, dig out mortises, and clean up joints. Jobs such as smoothing surfaces and squaring up boards call for a plane. For sophisticated edge treatments and joinery, the portable electric router is your best bet.

CHISELS

Though a browse through tool catalogs will turn up many chisel styles, the woodworker can concentrate on the following three types, illustrated at right.

Bench (bevel-edged) chisels, with 4- to 6-inch-long blades, have side bevels to fit tight spots. Blade widths typically range from ¼ inch to 2 inches. A shorter version, the *butt chisel,* is often used for all-purpose chiseling; its plastic handle and steel cap can stand up to rough pounding.

Firmer (framing) chisels have squared-off sides and blades up to 11 inches long for heavy-duty notching and paring. Blade widths vary from ½ inch to 2 inches.

Mortise chisels, with their long, narrow, square-edged blades, are designed for carving out deep recesses. Typical blade widths range from ¼ to ½ inch.

What blade widths are best? A good size to start with is ¾ inch; a ¼-inch blade is a good second choice.

■ *Chiseling tips.* To drive a butt, firmer, or mortise chisel, you'll probably need a mallet. Start out with short, light taps and swing harder as required.

As a rule, turn the chisel bevel down to remove material quickly; for more controlled work or to finish up rougher cuts, turn it bevel up.

In general, woodworkers remove most of the waste fairly quickly, but as they near the cutting line, they nibble small bits, finishing with hand pres-

Basic Chisel Types

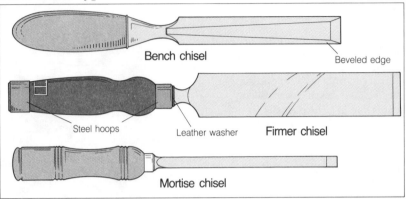

Bench chisel • Beveled edge
Steel hoops • Leather washer • Firmer chisel
Mortise chisel

Four Chiseling Tips

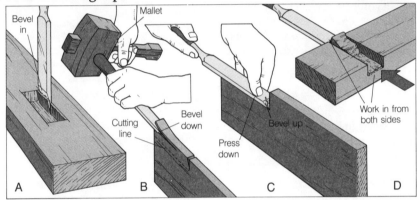

Bevel in • Mallet • Cutting line • Bevel down • Press down • Bevel up • Work in from both sides

A B C D

For clean chiseling, *use these techniques: keep the bevel facing in toward the waste when mortising or notching (A); remove waste quickly with the chisel bevel down (B); smooth to the line with the bevel up (C); to avoid splintering, cut in from both sides (D).*

sure alone. The very last, smoothing passes are made with the chisel perfectly flat or vertical, with your thumb pressing firmly down on the blade just behind the bevel, as shown above.

When chiseling through a board, don't break all the way through; instead, reverse the work and cut in from that side.

PLANES

Planes that woodworkers commonly use fall into two basic categories: bench and block planes. Bench planes smooth and square in line with the grain. Three main types are the *smoothing plane* (about 9¾ inches long with a 2-inch-wide blade), the *jack plane* (14 by 2 inches), and the *jointer plane* (22 by 2⅜ inches).

The shorter block planes (typically 6 by 1⅝ inches) smooth end grain, cut bevels and chamfers, and trim small bits of material from pieces that don't fit snugly. Unlike bench planes, they're designed to be operated with one hand.

To square-up a board, follow this sequence: (1) level the best face; (2) square-up one edge to the good face; (3) plane the other face; (4) true the second edge; and (5) square-up the ends.

Leveling a board's face. You can use a smoothing, jack, or jointer plane for this job. Whichever you opt for, adjust the blade depth for a fine cut. Grip the

Elements of Common Planes

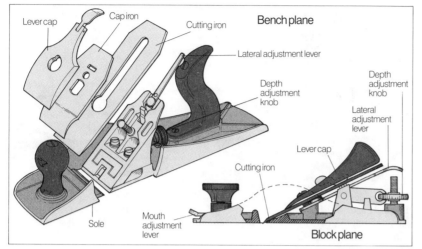

Planing a Face

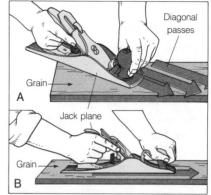

To level a board's face, *first make diagonal passes (A); then finish up in line with the grain (B).*

Truing an Edge

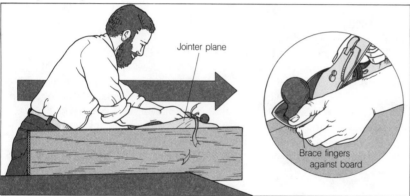

Planing the edge *of a long board requires a wide, balanced stance and continuous passes. Walk with each pass, if necessary, and guide the plane with the fingers of your leading hand (see inset).*

Squaring Up an End

End-grain work *is the block plane's specialty; a scrap block clamped to the edge keeps it from splitting.*

rear handle with one hand and the front knob with the other.

Work diagonally across the board, first in one direction and then in the other. If the board is very rough, set the blade for a deeper cut and overlap your passes.

Then place the blade of a square on the surface of the board: any light that shows beneath the blade indicates a low spot. Shade in the adjacent high spots with a pencil and plane the pencilled areas only. When the board is basically flat, set the plane for a very fine setting and plane directly with the grain.

Truing an edge. To square-up an edge, use the longest bench plane you

have—the longer sole will bridge low spots rather than ride up and down irregularities.

Begin by sighting down the edge and marking obvious high spots with a pencil; plane these first. Then, gripping the plane as shown above, work down the edge. Watch out for "dipping"—overplaning the ends of the board; instead, press on the front knob as you begin each stroke, even out the weight in the middle, and bear down on the handle as you finish.

Squaring up the ends. Hold a sharp block plane in one hand, applying pressure with your forefinger as necessary. Use short, shearing strokes, holding the plane at a slight angle to the

direction you're working. To prevent splitting the far edge, plane inward from both edges, or clamp scrap wood to the far edge, as shown above.

THE ELECTRIC ROUTER

A router equipped with the proper bit cuts all kinds of grooves—dadoes, rabbets, V-grooves, and even exact dovetails. It can also round or model the edges of a board, trim plastic laminate at a single pass, and whisk out mortises with the aid of a template. It pays to spend a little extra for a router that has at least a 1-horsepower motor; otherwise, the depth of cut possible in one pass is very limited.

SHAPING TOOLS

For occasional use, router bits made from high-speed steel are sufficient. Carbide-tipped bits cost more but stay sharp much longer—they're a must for hardwoods, particleboard, hardboard, and plastic laminates. When dull, they can be resharpened. The most popular bits, and the profiles they cut, are illustrated below.

Basic operation. The exact mechanism for setting bit depth varies from one router to the next; this setup may or may not be reliable. Happily, you can ensure an accurate setting on any router by simply measuring the depth between the bit and the baseplate; always test the setting on a piece of scrap.

Because the router bit spins in a clockwise direction, the router tends to drift or kick back counterclockwise in your hands. To compensate, you normally operate the router from *left to right*, so the cutter's leading edge always bites into new wood. Be sure to wear safety goggles.

Ready to cut? Grip the router securely by the handles, lining it up just outside the area to be cut. Turn the router on and let the motor reach full

Two Straight Cuts with the Router

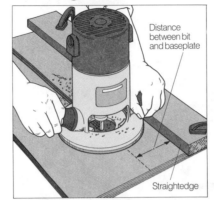

To guide a straight cut *inside a piece, clamp a straightedge to the stock for the router's baseplate to follow.*

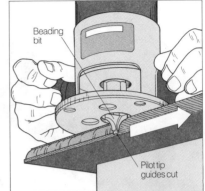

A pilot tip steers *the router's edge-shaping bits; for best results, move the router along the edges from left to right.*

speed; then carefully feed the bit into the work.

Take a look at the cuts you're producing: if the edges are ragged, you're cutting too fast; if they're burned, you're moving too slowly. Listen for the sound of the router's motor that corresponds to the smoothest cut, and you'll have little trouble.

Guiding the cut. For clean cuts *near an edge,* use the edge guide available for most router models. To guide cuts *inside a piece,* use a straightedge

clamped to the left of the cutting line. To locate it, measure the distance from the bit's outside edge to the edge of the baseplate; or make a test cut against the straightedge and check the distance from cut to guide.

For *edge-shaping,* choose a self-piloting router bit that indexes right off the edge being shaped. If you're shaping all four sides, begin with the end grain on one side. If you're routing the ends only, work from the edges *in* to prevent the end grain from splitting as the bit exits.

Elements of a Router

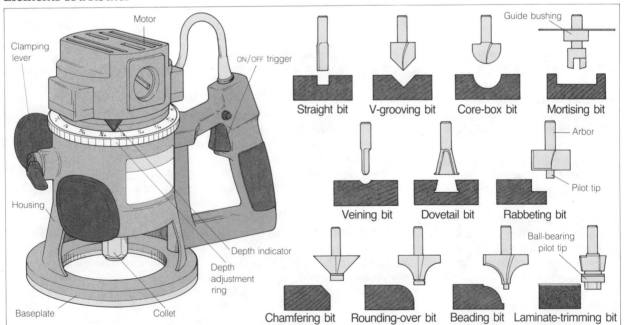

CONVERTIBLE SPACE-SAVER

In many city homes, storage space is limited, but creative planning can result in such sleek and efficient solutions as this wall system. Doubled ¾-inch plywood lends strength and substance; solid 1 by 2 lumber hides plywood edges. The counter-top slides out on drawer glides to become a desk (see detail photo at left). Design: John A.L. Jones.

DRILLING

Woodworkers drill holes for screws, bolts, dowels, drawer pulls, and hinges—even for nails in hardwoods. And a drill fitted with a screwdriver bit is a real boon for driving screws. Here's how to choose—and use—a drill for neat results.

THE PORTABLE ELECTRIC DRILL

The portable electric drill has virtually replaced its manual counterparts. A reliable model, with matching bits, costs little more than a good hand brace, and, with the right attachments, it's much more versatile.

Choosing a drill. An electric drill is classified by the maximum-size bit shank accommodated in its chuck. Three sizes are common: ¼ inch, ⅜ inch, and ½ inch. As chuck size increases, so does power output, or *torque*. But the higher the torque, the slower the speed. For most woodworking, the ⅜-inch drill offers the best compromise between power and speed; it also accepts a wide range of bits and accessories.

Single-speed, two-speed, and variable-speed models are available. A variable-speed drill, such as the one shown at right, lets you suit the speed to the job—very handy when starting holes or driving screws. Reversible gears help you remove screws and stuck bits.

If you'd rather not fumble with extension cords just to drill a few holes, the cordless electric drill, powered by a rechargeable battery pack, is a popular alternative. Some models can bore hundreds of holes or drive hundreds of screws on a single charge, and then recharge in an hour.

Drill bits. Tool catalogues and hardware stores are crammed with special drill bits. Here's a selection of the most reliable and most commonly used attachments.

Fractional twist bits, originally designed for drilling metal, are commonly used in wood. Sizes range from

The Electric Drill & Basic Bits

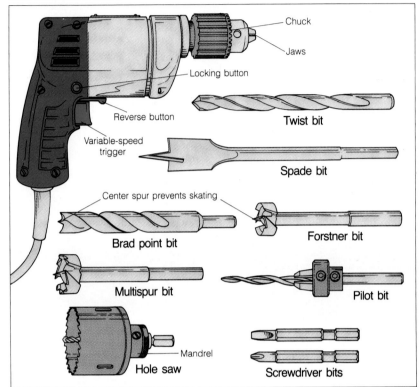

Chuck

Jaws

Locking button

Reverse button

Variable-speed trigger

Twist bit

Spade bit

Center spur prevents skating

Brad point bit

Forstner bit

Multispur bit

Pilot bit

Mandrel

Hole saw

Screwdriver bits

---

¹⁄₁₆ to ½ inch; sets are graduated by 32nds or 64ths. For durability, choose high-speed steel bits. Standard twist bits have shanks that correspond to each tip diameter; oversize twist bits have ¼- or ⅜-inch shanks but drill holes up to ½ inch. Long-shank twist bits handle deep drilling chores.

Spade bits, typically sized from ⅜ inch to 1½ inches, drill larger holes; the center spur prevents the "skating" common with twist bits. Spade bits leave fairly ragged holes, however, so you may not want to use them if the holes they drill will be visible or will have to be fitted with hardware, plugs, or dowels.

When appearance really counts, *brad point, Forstner,* or *multispur* bits are preferred, because they make cleaner holes than either twist or spade bits. They're also more costly. Brad point bits are available from ⅛ inch to an over-size ½ inch; both Forstner and multispur bits range from about ⅜ inch to 2 inches. Forstner bits are tops

for boring clean, flat-bottomed holes; both Forstner and multispur bits can bore holes in any direction, regardless of the wood grain.

For the largest holes, up to 4 inches, the solution is a *hole saw.* Though the type with interchangeable cutting wheels is handy, individual hole saws with fixed blades are more reliable. You'll need a mandrel (arbor) attachment, as shown above, to fit your drill chuck; the hole saw snaps onto the mandrel.

A *pilot bit* drills the proper pilot hole for a screw's threads, a larger hole for its shank, and a countersink (see facing page) for its head—all in one operation. Individual bits are more reliable than adjustable types. Typical sizes match screws from ¾ inch by #6 to 2 inches by #12.

Standard and Phillips *screwdriver bits* transform your electric drill into a power screwdriver, a very welcome tool when you have lots of screws to install. A two-speed or variable-speed

Drilling Straight Holes

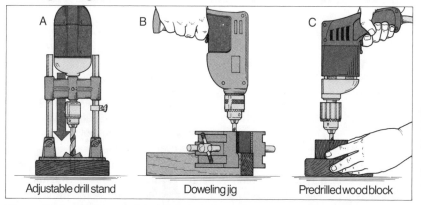

Three aids for drilling straight holes *include an adjustable drill stand, best for drilling a board's face (A); a doweling jig that centers holes on edges and ends (B); and a predrilled wood block (C).*

Gauging Depth

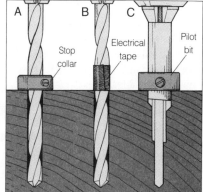

To drill to the right depth, *use a stop collar (A), wrap electrical tape around the bit (B), or try a pilot bit (C).*

drill is a must for these attachments—screws must be started and finished slowly or they'll strip.

DRILLING TIPS

When possible, clamp materials before drilling, particularly when using a ⅜- or ½-inch drill. If your drill allows, match the speed to the job: higher speeds for small bits and softwoods, slower speeds for large bits and hardwoods or metal. As you drill, apply only light pressure, letting the bit do the work. Leave the motor running as you remove the bit from the wood. Be sure to wear safety goggles.

When drilling large holes in hardwoods—especially with oversize twist bits— first make a small lead hole. Back the larger bit out occasionally to cool it and to clear stock from the hole.

Special problems. Three main problems plague the drilling process: centering the moving bit on its mark, drilling a perpendicular—or correctly angled—hole, and keeping the back surface from breaking away as the drill bit pierces. Here are some time-tested techniques for avoiding these pitfalls.

Use a pointed tool as a center punch when starting holes. An awl hole or a couple of taps with a hammer and nail or punch will prevent the bit from wandering.

A portable drill press is helpful for guiding an electric drill when you have

a lot of drilling to do, but a drill stand, (shown above), especially the type that adjusts for angles, is more convenient. Self-centering doweling jigs are quite accurate for drilling edges and end grain. Homespun methods include drilling a wood block and then using it as a guide, or simply lining up the drill body with the help of a square.

To keep the back side of the wood from breaking away, either clamp a wood scrap to the back of your work piece and drill through the piece into the scrap or, just as the bit's center spur pierces, flip the piece over and finish drilling from the other side.

How do you stop a bit at a specific depth? Buy a stop collar, wrap tape around the bit at the correct depth, or use a pilot bit.

Countersinking and counterboring. Drywall screws, when driven with an electric drill and screwdriver bit, usually don't need a pilot hole in softwoods. In harder materials, use a ³⁄₃₂-inch bit for #6 screws and a ⅛-inch bit for #8 screws. Drill two-thirds to three-quarters the screw's length.

For woodscrews, pick a drill bit the diameter of the screw's shank and drill only as deep as the length of the unthreaded shank. In hardwoods, also drill a smaller hole—about half as deep as the threaded portion is long—for the threads below the shank hole. Use a bit slightly smaller in diameter than the core between the threads.

Drywall and flathead woodscrews are normally countersunk to sit flush with the surface. But sometimes, the screw is sunk even deeper, or counterbored, and then covered with wood putty or a plug. To drill these holes, choose either a second bit (⁵⁄₁₆ inch for #6 drywall screws, ⅜ inch for #8) or a pilot bit, which creates pilot, countersink, and counterbore in one operation. Unless you're using the pilot bit, drill the countersink or counterbore hole *first* and then add the pilot hole in the center.

Machine bolts and lag screws look best when counterbored. Drill the counterbore hole first, using a bit that's the same diameter as the washer behind the bolt head or nut. Then drill the hole for the shaft down the center.

Pilot Hole Profile

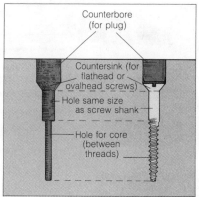

Predrilling *saves both screws and aching muscles.*

Because the art of fastening—like measuring and cutting—is fundamental to woodworking, you should become well versed in the tools that make it possible.

HAMMERS

When you choose the right hammer and know a few basic techniques, you'll reap immediate benefits in the form of fewer bent nails; you'll also save wear and tear on your wood and on your fingers.

Claw hammer. This basic hammer is available in two main types: *curved claw* and *ripping claw*. The curved claw offers leverage for nail pulling and allows you to swing in tight spots. The ripping claw, which is fairly straight, is chiefly designed to pull or rip pieces apart.

Notice that hammer faces may be either flat or slightly convex. The convex, or bell-faced, type allows you to drive a nail flush without marring the wood's surface. Mesh-type faces are available for rough framing, but don't use these for fine work—the pattern will show.

Head weights range from 7 to 28 ounces. For general work, many woodworkers choose a 16-ounce curved-claw hammer. Though handles made from steel or fiberglass are stronger, many woodworkers still prefer the feel of wood—hickory and ash are tops.

Basic nailing techniques. As a rule, choose a nail that's two to three times as long as the thickness of the top board you're nailing. To start a nail, hold it between your thumb and forefinger and give it a few light taps with a hammer. Once the nail is started,

remove your fingers and swing more fully, combining wrist, arm, and shoulder action.

If you bend a nail, remove it with the hammer's claw—a scrap block between the hammer and the wood protects the surface. It's easy to split hardwoods; to avoid this, drill pilot holes when nailing near an edge.

Drive finishing nails to within ⅛ inch of the surface, beginning with full hammer strokes and ending with short, careful taps. Then tap the nail head below the surface with the point of a *nailset* (shown below, at left). You can conceal the resulting hole with wood putty.

SCREWDRIVERS

The lowly screwdriver vies with the hammer as the most frequently employed tool in a do-it-yourselfer's collection. Yet many prospective woodworkers don't know the fine points of selecting and using screwdrivers.

A basic selection. Screwdrivers fall into two main categories: *standard* and *Phillips*. Shank lengths of standard screwdrivers range from about 3 to 12 inches; corresponding tip widths vary from ⅛ to ⅜ inch. Stock up on three or four sizes covering the range and then add a *stubby*—typically 1½ inches long—for work in close quarters. For fine finish work, look for *cabinet tips*, which have flattened, parallel shapes.

Phillips screwdrivers are sized by shank length (up to 8 inches) and tip number, ranging from 0 (the smallest) to 4. A set containing sizes 1, 2, and 3 should answer most needs.

Offset screwdrivers help you reach tight spots. The models with one standard and one Phillips tip give you two tools in one.

Spiral-ratchet screwdrivers, accepting a variety of tips, are handsavers when you need to drive large quantities of screws by hand. The chuck turns as the handle is pushed down.

Screwdriver bits for an electric drill (see page 32) also save energy. You'll

(Continued on page 39)

Two Claw Hammers... & a Nailset

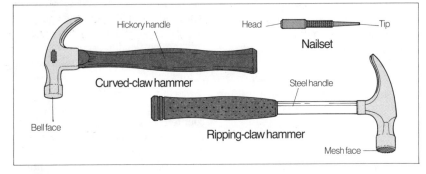

Hickory handle · Head · Tip · Nailset · Curved-claw hammer · Steel handle · Bell face · Ripping-claw hammer · Mesh face

Screwdrivers: A Selection

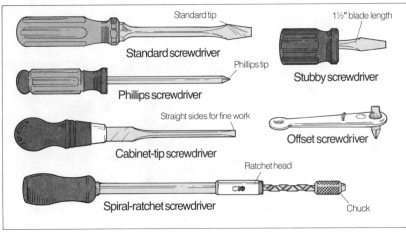

Standard tip · 1½" blade length · Standard screwdriver · Phillips tip · Stubby screwdriver · Phillips screwdriver · Straight sides for fine work · Offset screwdriver · Cabinet-tip screwdriver · Ratchet head · Spiral-ratchet screwdriver · Chuck

AUDIO-VIDEO CORNER

Gleaming with a classic red stain finish, this mahogany corner system neatly accommodates a collection of state-of-the-art electronic equipment. For stability and solid good looks, the shelves are faced with 1 by 2 lips. Rounded edges and decorative molding at the top contribute traditional elegance. Housed in its own little niche is a pull-out ottoman for serious relaxation. Design: Osburn Design.

THE ART
OF
JOINERY

Joinery—the craft of assembling pieces of wood accurately and securely—is a crucial step for the success of your project. The use and construction of all the basic cabinetmaker's joints are outlined below.

Butt joints

To make a simple butt joint, where two boards butt up against one another, the mating surfaces must be square, smooth, and flat. Then you butt one board against the other, fastening them with glue only or with glue plus screws or nails.

Blind-doweling reinforces weak flat and edge joints. The trick is drilling straight, matching holes in each piece. A self-centering doweling jig (see page 33) makes the whole process much easier. Otherwise, lay the surfaces face to face and mark across both pieces. Drill both holes slightly deeper than half the dowel length.

Miter joints

A miter joint—two pieces cut and joined at a 45° angle—is used mainly to hide end grain at corners. There are two versions: flat and on-edge.

Radial-arm and table saws have adjustable blades and guides that make mitering simpler. If you're cutting miters with a handsaw, a miter box (see page 20) will help you enormously.

Dado joints

Dadoes—U-shaped grooves cut on a board's face—make strong, rigid joints; they're widely used to build drawers and to join shelves or partitions to bookcase or cabinet frames. A dado that's a quarter to a third the board's thickness is enough—never exceed one-half.

Power tools work best for cutting dadoes. An electric router equipped with a straight bit smooths the cut as it goes. For a cut near an edge, use the router's edge guide; otherwise, clamp a straightedge onto the work for the baseplate to follow.

To cut dadoes with a standard power saw blade, set the blade at the correct depth, cut the borders (using a fence or guide), and make repeated passes through the waste wood until it falls out. Finish each groove with light chisel strokes. Dado heads, available for both table and radial-arm saws, can cut a dado in one pass.

The recess doesn't show in a *stopped* dado. To make one, cut the dado only partway; notch the other piece to fit.

Rabbet joints

Rabbets, grooves cut along board edges, are commonly used for corners. Rabbets are stronger than butt joints and also minimize the amount of visible end and edge grain. Generally, the rabbet's width is the same as the thickness of the stock; the depth is up to half that.

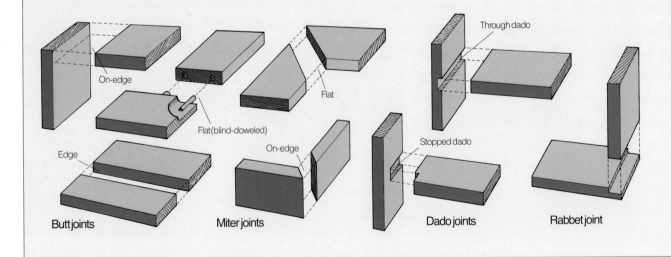

On-edge

Flat (blind-doweled)

Flat

Edge

On-edge

Through dado

Stopped dado

Butt joints

Miter joints

Dado joints

Rabbet joint

It's nearly impossible to execute a long rabbet with a handsaw. Instead, use a router fitted with either a self-piloting rabbeting bit or a standard straight bit and scrap guide; or turn to a stationary power saw equipped with a dado head or standard blade. If you're using the standard blade, cut the inside border first; then remove the waste as described on the facing page for dado joints.

A *rabbet-and-dado* joint combines both joints in one and can be used in place of either for extra strength. It's particularly effective for plywood cabinets.

Lap joints

Both end-lap and cross-lap joints are useful in cabinetry. To make end-laps, cut identical rabbets in both pieces, each as wide as the stock and exactly half its thickness.

Cross-laps require matching notches: the width of each notch should be exactly the same as the thickness of the connecting piece; the depth should be half the width of the connecting piece. Cut the sides of each notch with a hand or power saw; finish off the bottom with a chisel, coping saw, or saber saw.

Mortise & tenon joints

Cabinetmakers use mortise and tenon joints for strong connections in cabinet faceframes and frame-and-panel doors. Two common versions are the blind mortise and the open mortise. For either type, plan to make both the mortise and matching tenon one-third the thickness of the stock. You can cut a blind mortise with a mortising chisel alone, but it's faster to drill out the waste first, using a drill bit that matches the mortise width. It's even simpler to use a router equipped with a straight bit and a template or jig. Open mortises can be drilled out from the side and finished with vertical saw cuts; or cut all at once with a table or radial-arm saw, a dado head, and a tenoning jig.

The matching tenon is cut like a wide rabbet, except that you make the cut on two or four sides. The fit of the tenon in the mortise should be snug, but you should be able to push the tenon in with few mallet taps.

Dovetail joints

Strong, decorative dovetails are the traditional way to join drawer sides and other boxlike structures. For centuries, dovetails were made with a handsaw and chisel only; today, most woodworkers rely on a router and dovetail bit, and a dovetail fixture. Some fixtures cut flush dovetails only; others produce *through* dovetails (where pins show on both sides).

The box (finger) joint can be cut either by hand or with a table saw fitted with a dado head, and some type of homemade jig to hold the stock upright and regulate the pin spacing.

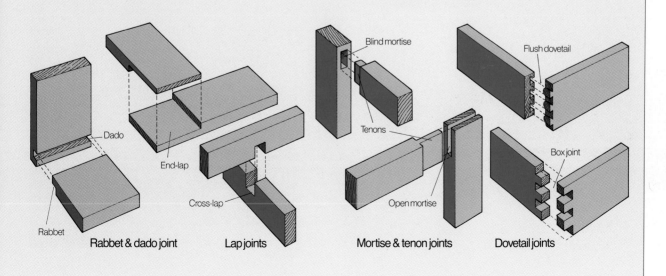

Dado · End-lap · Cross-lap · Rabbet

Rabbet & dado joint · Lap joints

Blind mortise · Tenons · Open mortise · Flush dovetail · Box joint

Mortise & tenon joints · Dovetail joints

REDWOOD RETREAT

Sturdy redwood shelves support a library in this inviting corner. Though made from 1-by lumber, the unit looks more substantial because the uprights are first paired, then capped with 1 by 4s (see detail at right). The adjustable shelves are lipped with 1 by 2s, so they appear heavier, too. The corner upright stands at a 45° angle, with shelves cut to fit. Design: John A.L. Jones.

FASTENING

need a two-speed or variable-speed drill for such a bit.

Tips on driving screws. When screwing through one board into the end grain of another, use a screw that's long enough so that about two-thirds its length will enter the bottom piece. If you're joining boards face to face, the screw should be ⅛ to ¼ inch shorter than the combined thicknesses. Screws usually require pilot holes. For drilling techniques, turn to pages 32–33.

If a screwdriver's tip is too large or too small for a screw's slot, it can burr the screw head or even slide off and gouge the work. Be sure to choose the right size screwdriver for the job. If the screw is stubborn, try rubbing soap or wax on the threads. If it still sticks, drill a larger or longer pilot hole.

WRENCHES

For fastening bolts and lag screws, turn to a wrench. For occasional use only, choose an *adjustable wrench*, good for a number of bolt or nut sizes. For general work, the 8-inch size, with a ¹⁵⁄₁₆-inch jaw capacity, is a good choice.

Individually sized *box* and *open-end wrenches* are kinder to nuts and bolts. A typical set ranges from ¼ inch to 1¼ inches.

A *ratchet and socket set* is a necessity for countersinking bolt heads and nuts. The ⅜-inch drive is the most versatile: socket sizes range from ⅜ to ¹³⁄₁₆ inch, in increments of ¹⁄₁₆ inch.

Driving bolts. To give the nut a firm bite, pick a bolt ½ inch longer than the combined thicknesses of the pieces being joined. (If you're countersinking or counterboring the head and/or nut, be sure to subtract these depths from the total.) To keep the nut from spinning while you tighten the head, hold it with a second wrench or ratchet.

Driving lag screws. To install a lag screw, first drill a pilot hole two-thirds the diameter and length of the screw; start the lag with a hammer and finish it with a wrench (if you're counterboring, use a ratchet and socket).

CLAMPS

Clamps hold assembled parts tight while glue sets and practically lend an extra pair of hands when you need help. A woodworker's tip: To protect wood surfaces from being marred by the jaws of a metal clamp, fit a scrap block between the jaws and the wood surface.

Clamps come in many shapes and sizes. Here's a selection:

Steel *C-clamps* are standard for small jobs—clamping localized areas, holding work to a bench or sawhorse, and attaching scrap guides for cutting. Common jaw widths range from 1 inch to 8 inches.

Spring clamps are suitable for quick clamping of light work and excel at fixing scrap guides. Designed like large clothespins, they have jaw capacities ranging from 1 inch to 3 inches; the 3-inch size is the most versatile.

The wooden jaws of a *hand screw* adjust for both depth and angle, and hold odd-shaped assemblies. Sizes range from 4 to 16 inches in length, with jaw capacities from 2 to 12 inches.

Bar and *pipe clamps* have one fixed and one sliding jaw for clamping across wide expanses. Bar clamps are commonly available in sizes from 6 to 36 inches, but some models are as long as 6 feet.

Pipe clamp fittings, attached to any length of ½- or ¾-inch black (nongalvanized) pipe, are much less expensive than bar clamps and can be tailored to suit the job at hand.

Wrenches for Woodworking

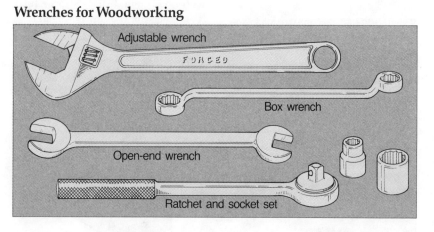

Adjustable wrench

FORGED

Box wrench

Open-end wrench

Ratchet and socket set

A Collection of Clamps

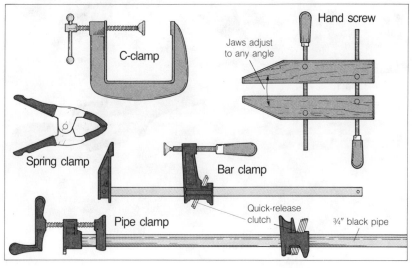

C-clamp

Hand screw

Jaws adjust to any angle

Spring clamp

Bar clamp

Pipe clamp

Quick-release clutch

¾" black pipe

Most projects require careful smoothing and finishing before they're ready to be presented to the world.

Smoothing means sanding or scraping. When it comes to sanding, the most common smoothing technique, you can choose between muscle power and electric power. Then it's on to the final steps—preparing the wood and applying the finish.

Here are the tools and techniques you'll need to successfully complete your project.

ABRASIVES

When preparing a wood surface for a fine finish, most woodworkers turn to a series of progressively finer sandpaper grades. Steel wool provides the final polish. Scraping is an alternative to sanding—many woodworkers feel that the resulting surface is smoother and takes finishes better. Whatever your choice, the tools and materials you'll need are discussed below.

Sandpaper. Sandpaper is sandpaper, right? Actually, it's not even made with sand. The material and type you use depend on the results you want to achieve.

Flint paper, beige in color, offers the least expensive but also the least durable and effective option.

Garnet paper, reddish to golden brown, provides excellent results for hand-sanding, especially in the final stages.

Aluminum oxide, light gray to grayish brown, is a synthetic material of great toughness; choose it for rough to medium hand-sanding and for a power sander's belt or pad.

Silicon carbide, blue gray to charcoal, is often called *wet-or-dry* because its waterproof backing allows you to use it wet, thus eliminating the clogging tendency of its tiny grains. Try it as a final "polish" on wood or to cut excess gloss between finish coats.

Sandpaper type is usually labeled on the sheet's backing. Other information you'll find there includes grit number, backing weight, and the distinction *open coat* or *closed coat.*

Grit numbers run from a low of 12 up to 600, but 50 (very coarse) to 220 (very fine) is the common range. Wet-or-dry paper is generally available up to 600-grit.

Backing weight is rated from A (thinnest) to E. In general, backing weight decreases as grit becomes finer.

Closed-coat sandpaper has more particles to cut faster, but it clogs in soft materials; open coat works better for rough sanding.

To provide a flat surface for your sandpaper, use a *sanding block.* You can buy one or you can make your own by wrapping sandpaper around a wood block faced with a ½-inch-thick pad of felt or sponge rubber.

■ *Sanding tips.* To prepare for a fine finish, divide sanding into at least three stages: rough-sand with 50- to 80-grit paper; switch to 120-grit for a second sanding; then sand once more with 180- to 220-grit paper. Some materials and finishes may require a fourth pass with even finer paper or with 3/0 or 4/0 steel wool.

On end grain, move straight across in one direction only to avoid rounding the edges and clogging the wood pores.

Steel wool. Purchased in the form of pads and in many grades, steel wool is popular among wood finishers as a mild abrasive. Grades 2/0 and 3/0 are finely textured and are often used for final surface polishing before finish application. The very fine texture of grade 4/0 is perfect for smoothing between finish coats.

Scrapers. *Hand scrapers* appear to be simple steel cutouts, but look closer—the hooked edges produce fine shavings when pushed or pulled in line with wood grain. To use a scraper, hold it upright, with your fingers behind; bow the blade in with finger pressure, rock the scraper toward you slightly, and pull it along the board.

A cabinet scraper has a frame with two handles, making scraping less fatiguing and more consistent.

Smoothing Tools

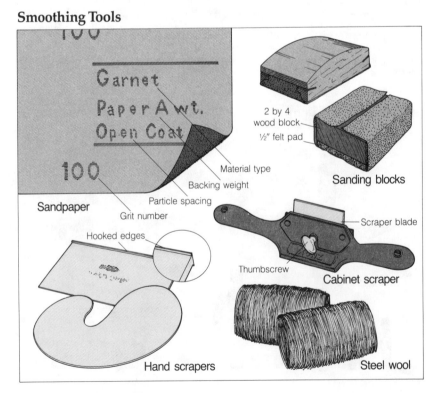

Sandpaper
Garnet Paper A wt. Open Coat
100
Material type
Backing weight
Particle spacing
Grit number
Hooked edges
Hand scrapers

2 by 4 wood block
½" felt pad
Sanding blocks

Scraper blade
Thumbscrew
Cabinet scraper
Steel wool

Power Sanders

Portable electric sanders fall into two main categories: belt and finishing sanders (see illustration at right). A belt sander provides the needed clout for leveling and cleaning up minor dents and scratches, lumber stamps, or scribed lines. Finishing sanders work at very high speeds to produce a finer, more controlled finish; they're great for intermediate and final sanding.

Belt sanders. Sized by the width and length of the belt, the most popular belt sander sizes are 3 by 21, 3 by 24, and 4 by 24 inches. Features to look for include a dust-collection system, as well as convenient methods of replacing the belt and adjusting belt tracking.

Belt coarseness was originally rated by fractions, from 4¼ (coarsest) to 0 (medium) to 10/0 (finest), but today you'll normally see grit numbers like those on sandpaper sheets. Common belt grits range from 36 to 120.

To fit a belt to your sander, release the lever that slackens the front roller, install the new belt with the arrow on the backing pointing in the clockwise direction, and tighten the lever. Use the tracking control knob to center the belt on the roller.

When using a belt sander, remember two basic rules: clamp small materials down and always keep the sander moving when it's in contact with the work. Belt sanders can remove a lot of material quickly.

Move the sander forward and back in line with the grain. At the end of each pass, lift it up and repeat, overlapping the previous pass by half. Don't apply pressure—the weight of the sander alone is sufficient.

Finishing sanders. Though most finishing sanders have either straight-line or orbital action, some allow you to switch from one motion to the other. Straight-line action theoretically produces a finer finish, but an orbital sander also gives good results.

Finishing sanders range from 4 by 4⅜ inches (pad size) to about 4½ by 9⅝ inches. The smallest sizes, designed to be held in one hand, allow you to sand

Elements of Power Sanders

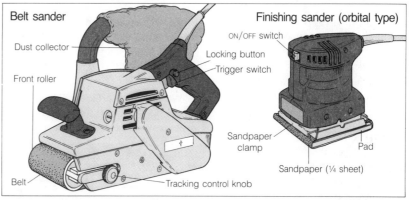

Belt sander

Dust collector

Front roller

Belt

Tracking control knob

Finishing sander (orbital type)

ON/OFF switch

Locking button

Trigger switch

Sandpaper clamp

Pad

Sandpaper (¼ sheet)

vertical and overhead surfaces comfortably. Be sure the sander you choose takes exactly a quarter, a third, or half of a standard sandpaper sheet.

To load your sander, slide one end of the paper under the clamp on one side, stretch the sheet tightly, and clamp the other end.

Both straight-line and orbital types work best when moved in line with the wood grain. For a fine finish, you may still have to sand the corners and edges by hand.

Brushes, Rollers & Pads

Applying a fine finish requires only a few additional tools (shown below). Here's a quick rundown.

Paintbrushes. For best results, be sure to select the correct bristle type and size of brush.

Natural bristles (Chinese boar, ox, or badger hair) are traditionally used to apply oil-base finishes. They should not be used with water-base products (such as latex paint)—the bristles quickly become soggy.

Synthetic bristles (nylon or nylonlike) are best for water-base finishes.

How do you pick a first-rate brush? Price is one indication. Another rule: The longer and thicker a brush for its width, the better. Bounce the bristles against the back of your hand—quality bristles feel soft and springy. Fan them with your hand to see if any come loose; loss of one or two is normal, but more means trouble. Be sure the bristle tips are "flagged" (split and frayed).

Stick with brushes from 1 to 3 inches wide. The 1-inch brush is good for edges and delicate trim; use the 3-inch version for large, flat surfaces.

Rollers and pads. A 3-inch-wide paint roller lays on enamel quickly and

Accessories for a Fine Finish

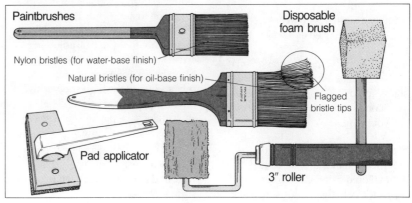

Paintbrushes

Nylon bristles (for water-base finish)

Natural bristles (for oil-base finish)

Pad applicator

Disposable foam brush

Flagged bristle tips

3" roller

smoothly. A pad applicator, which resembles a sponge attached to a short handle, is even simpler to use. If cleanup isn't your strong suit, look for disposable foam "brushes," which produce similar results.

FINISHING TIPS

Ready to finish? First, you'll need to repair any surface flaws, finish-sand, and seal and stain as required. Then it's on to the top coat—oil, shellac, lacquer, varnish, or enamel. Below, you'll find pointers on all of these steps. (For the characteristics of the various finishing products, see page 14.)

Filling and patching. Cracks, hammer marks, and fastener holes should be filled with wood putty before finish-sanding. Spread wood putty with a putty knife or, for nail holes, with your finger. Build up each patch slightly above the surface and then sand it level. When filling larger or deep holes, build up the patch in layers.

If you're planning to paint, the color of the patch isn't critical. But for a clear finish, pick a putty the same shade as the wood. If you'll be staining, patch with the same color as the final finish. To be sure you have the best combination, test the putty and stain on a scrap of the same wood.

Sealing. A sealer is sometimes applied to sanded wood—especially softwoods and Douglas fir plywood—before stain or clear finish coats. Its primary job is to reduce moisture absorption so that finish coats go on more evenly.

Shellac diluted with denatured alcohol is often used as a sealer. You'll also find a variety of special products in home improvement centers. Since sealers react differently with various stains and materials, be sure to test your combination on a wood scrap or ask your dealer.

Staining. Though many woods require no stain at all, nondescript, light-colored wood gains color and character from the application of stain.

Pigmented oil and penetrating oil stains are easy to use: simply apply them with a brush (a disposable foam brush works well) or a rag. Wipe off pigmented oil stain immediately; allow penetrating oil to soak in, and then wipe off and buff.

Water stains tend to swell wood fibers. To counteract this tendency, first wet the wood with warm water; then sand swollen areas before staining. Let the stain dry for at least 24 hours.

Because they're so quick drying, it's best to spray on non-grain-raising stains. You can add a retarder to such a stain to make it brushable.

Applying an oil finish. Penetrating resin is the most foolproof clear finish around. Typically, you just spread penetrating resin on the bare wood with a brush or rag, wait half an hour, and wipe off the excess surface liquid with a clean rag. A second—even a third— application is usually a good idea, especially if the wood is very porous. If you'd like greater surface luster or extra protection, apply two or more coats of paste wax.

Tung oil will never develop a high gloss, but its sheen does increase with each coat. Rub the oil into the wood with a soft cloth. Apply at least two coats, 24 hours apart, and then buff with a lambswool pad.

Using shellac. Though shellac is typically sold in 3- or 4-pound *cuts* (the higher the cut, the stronger the shellac), a 1- or 2-pound cut is best for beginners. To make a 1-pound cut from a 4-pound one, add 3 parts denatured alcohol to 1 part shellac.

Like tung oil, a shellac finish requires several layers before it begins to take on luster. Apply the first coat with a slow, smooth motion, taking special care to overlap all adjoining brush strokes and to maintain a clean, smooth surface. After an hour or so, rub or sand off the high spots with 320-grit sandpaper or steel wool. (If the shellac clogs the paper, wait a few more minutes before sanding.)

Apply the second and third coats in the same way. Then use 4/0 steel wool and paraffin oil to even up the surface gloss.

If you're after a classic high-gloss look, allow at least 3 days for the new finish to harden; then polish with pumice or rottenstone. Follow with wax.

Applying lacquer. Though professionals usually apply lacquer with a spray gun, special brushing lacquers also produce good results.

Working rapidly with a wider than normal brush to speed things along, brush on lacquer liberally, using long strokes. Keep your working area small and finish one area before moving on to the next.

Let the lacquer dry for at least 4 hours; then carefully level any high spots or defects with 400-grit sandpaper. After the final coat has dried overnight (two coats are the bare minimum), you can rub the surface with pumice or rottenstone and oil for an even higher gloss.

Finishing with varnish. This category includes alkyd, spar, and polyurethane varnishes. Apply all three types by brushing first with the grain and then against; then smooth out with the grain one last time. To avoid runs, drips, and a thick "plastic" look, use varnish sparingly, building up two or three light coats.

After letting the varnish dry for at least 24 hours, use 400-grit sandpaper to provide better adhesion for the next coat. To cut excess gloss, rub the final coat with steel wool.

Laying on enamel. Always start your paint job with an undercoat, or primer. Not only does the undercoat seal the wood (allowing finish coats to go on much more easily), but it also helps point up any remaining surface flaws, which can then be puttied or sanded. After priming, smooth the surface with 220-grit sandpaper.

Brush the enamel generously onto the wood and then feather it out with lighter strokes in the direction of the grain. Or, for larger areas, use a 3-inch paint roller and smooth it out with light brush strokes.

Let the first finish coat dry (refer to the can for drying times); then sand lightly with 320- or 400-grit sandpaper before applying a second, final coat.

EUROPEAN ELEGANCE

Sophisticated storage unit attractively combines birch and plastic laminate. The shelves and uprights, reinforced with solid-lumber facings, show off the striking patterns of birch plywood. The countertop and doors are faced with durable plastic laminate. Mounted on invisible hinges and banded with solid birch (see at left), the doors cover the entire cabinet front in classic European style. Design: Osburn Design.

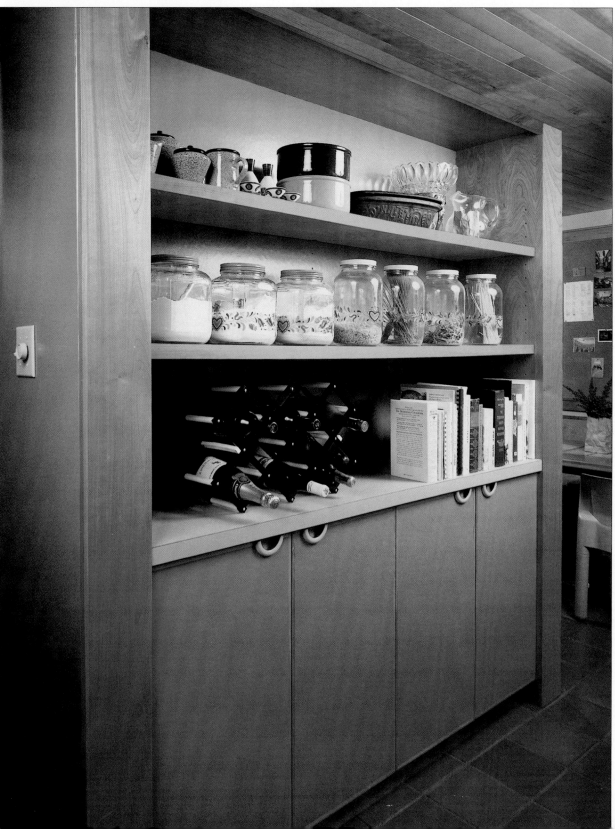

DESIGN
&
ASSEMBLY

In this chapter, we turn to specifics — open shelves, a bookcase, faceframe cabinets, doors, and drawers. In each case, we present general guidelines for design, dimensions, and joinery, then walk you through the cutting and assembly sequences. Special features along the way outline the construction of European-style cabinets and custom countertops. Finally, we'll show you how to install your new project.

Don't worry if some aspects of design or assembly seem over your head. In addition to featuring many of the same techniques the pros use, we offer alternatives for those with more modest tools or experience. If you have questions about a particular material, tool, or technique, be sure to refer back to the earlier chapters for help.

Also take the time to look at the shelves and cabinets around you. Analyze their design, take measurements, and examine the joinery. You'll learn a lot — and it may provide inspiration for your next project.

Bookshelf Basics

Shelf building is largely a matter of horizontals and verticals. Below, we take a look at both shelf construction (the horizontals) and classic support methods (the verticals).

Shelf Engineering

The drawing below shows five basic ways to make a shelf. The one you choose will depend on the appearance you want, the load your shelves will carry, and the distance they'll span between supports.

For light loads (small art objects, stemware, baskets), 1-by pine or fir supported every 32 inches works fine. For medium loads (books, glasses, some audio gear), shorten the span to 24 inches; you can also reinforce the edges with 1 by 2 lips, as shown. The maximum span for ¾-inch particleboard

is also 24 inches — it tends to sag under its own weight.

Most hardwoods and ¾-inch plywood will stay straight at 36 inches. Hide plywood edges with wood tape, lumber strips, or molding.

For longer spans or such heavy loads as wine racks, TVs, or large stereo rigs, use 2-by lumber; even stronger is a composite shelf made of two layers of plywood with reinforced edges. Two-by shelves can span 48 inches — longer if loads are light to medium.

For books of average size, allow at least 9 inches in height and 8 inches in depth. Larger volumes may require shelf space 12 inches high and deep. For record collections, figure 13 by 13 inches. TV and stereo units usually need 16 to 24 inches of depth. If you're building bookshelves, figure eight to ten books per running foot of shelf space.

Shelf Supports

You can hang shelves on the wall, prop them up off the floor, or suspend them from the ceiling. Here's a sampler of classic methods.

Quick and easy ideas. The simplest way to support shelves is to stack them. Try, for example, the student's perennial favorite — bricks and boards (see below). For a "cubbyhole" look, arrange boards between plastic or wooden crates — or even chimney flue tiles.

A windowsill shelf is a simple extension of the sill itself; just attach a wider board with countersunk woodscrews. For shelves over twice the original sill width, reinforce them with brackets or L-braces.

Ropes and chains hold shelves up like playground swings. Thread rope

Five Shelf Types

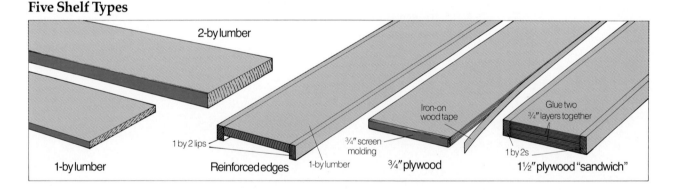

2-by lumber

1 by 2 lips

1-by lumber

Reinforced edges

1-by lumber

¾" screen molding

¾" plywood

Iron-on wood tape

Glue two ¾" layers together

1 by 2s

1½" plywood "sandwich"

Quick & Easy Shelving

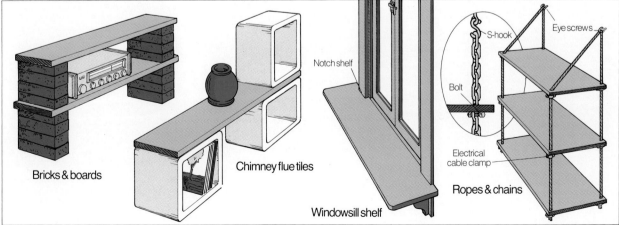

Bricks & boards

Chimney flue tiles

Notch shelf

Windowsill shelf

S-hook

Bolt

Eye screws

Electrical cable clamp

Ropes & chains

CEDAR & SOAPSUDS

Rich-looking cedar shelves provide out-in-the-open storage for towels, books, and a miniature folk art collection. Cedar stands up to water, a virtue that makes it ideal for use in bathrooms and kitchens. The smooth shelves, curved and notched to fit the alcove exactly, complement the rough-sawn cedar paneling and trim. Architect: William Abbott.

Bookshelf Basics

or chain through holes drilled in each shelf corner. Attach each unit to ceiling joists with eye screws.

Brackets. Brackets, braces, and metal angles can be purchased in a wide variety of sizes, styles, and finishes (for some examples, see below). Simply screw brackets to wall studs or use other wall fasteners, if necessary (see page 70). For both adjustability and ease of installation, manufactured tracks and brackets are a good choice.

Uprights. Many shelf units utilize some type of upright to support shelves from the side. The drawing at the bottom of the page shows a number of options.

Simple butt joints, glued and nailed or screwed, will suffice for light duty; they'll also do for heavier loads if you're using 2-by lumber. Cleats or L-brackets are stronger. Dadoed construction adds rigidity to backless units. If you want adjustable shelves, use pegs, pins, or tracks and clips.

What keeps the uprights upright? A ¼-inch plywood back is the sturdiest solution; otherwise, securely fasten the uprights to the ceiling or wall, or wedge them against the ceiling, using one of the methods shown in the inset drawing at the bottom of the page.

Brackets: An Assortment

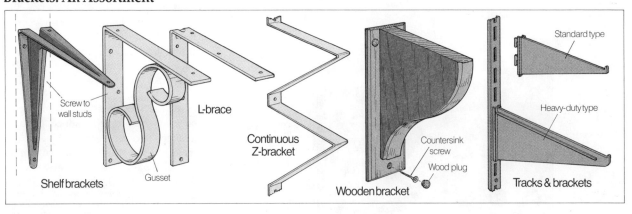

Screw to wall studs — Shelf brackets — Gusset — L-brace — Continuous Z-bracket — Countersink screw — Wood plug — Wooden bracket — Standard type — Heavy-duty type — Tracks & brackets

Ideas for Uprights

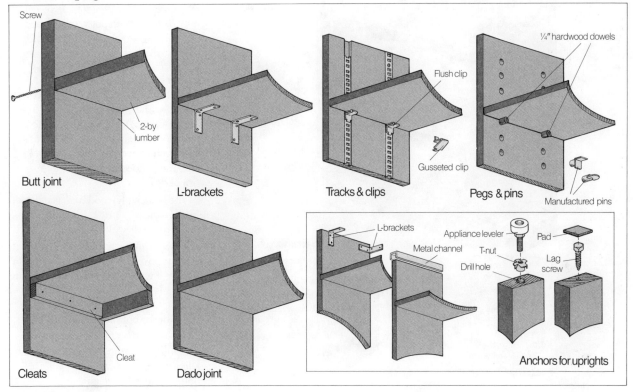

Screw — 2-by lumber — Butt joint — L-brackets — Flush clip — Tracks & clips — Gusseted clip — ¼" hardwood dowels — Pegs & pins — Manufactured pins — Cleat — Cleats — Dado joint — L-brackets — Metal channel — Appliance leveler — T-nut — Drill hole — Pad — Lag screw — Anchors for uprights

BUILDING A BOOKCASE

The most elegant home for your book collection is, of course, a formal bookcase. In this section, we'll show you how to design and build one.

DESIGN NOTES

A bookcase is essentially a box: the top, sides, and bottom define the space, and the back (like the bottom of the box) holds the case rigid and square. Though the basic components don't vary, you do have many choices in size, materials, shelving design, and joinery.

Dimensions. The only real restriction on your case size is shelf span, as discussed on page 45. If you're planning a wider case, simply add a vertical partition, as shown in the inset at left in the drawing below. For a unit that's both tall *and* wide, either build it in place or assemble smaller cases and screw them together once they're in position.

Materials. For most bookcases, standard dimension lumber works fine. Softwood 1 by 10s or 1 by 12s are economical choices, but 2-by lumber is stronger and adds a solid, furniture-like appearance. If the depth of your bookcase is greater than the width of a single board, either use plywood or edge-join smaller boards (see page 36).

You can use hardboard or plywood for the back; ⅛-inch hardboard is sufficient for small cases, but ¼-inch plywood is tops for both strength and appearance.

Shelves: fixed or adjustable? Fixed shelves—butt-joined, dadoed, or attached to cleats (see page 47)—will make the case stronger. If a case over 4 feet tall is made from 1-by softwood or ¾-inch plywood, it's best to fix at least one middle shelf.

Adjustable shelves are more flexible; support them with tracks and clips or with pegs. The tracks can be surface-mounted or, for a neater look, recessed into grooves. With pegs, you'll need two rows of ¼-inch holes in each side; see page 56 for details.

Joinery. The top, bottom, and sides of the bookcase shown at left are connected with simple rabbet joints (for other options, see pages 36–37). To join a fixed shelf or interior partition, use a dado joint. For a more finished look, stop the dadoes an inch from the front edge.

The ¼-inch plywood back is recessed inside a rabbet along the inside edges of the top, sides, and bottom.

A floor unit looks best if it rests on some type of *kickbase*. Make it from 2 by 4s; face it with better lumber or flooring materials once the unit is installed. Another option is to simply dado the sides for the bottom, leaving a 3-inch *kickspace* below.

If you're planning a heavy wall unit, add a *nail rail* (shown on page 53) to help support the weight.

Bookcase Components

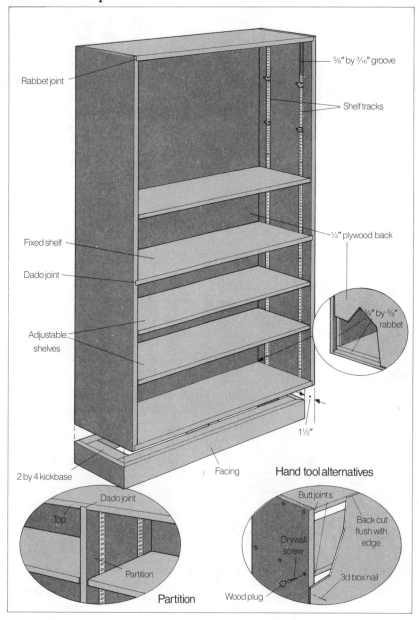

- Rabbet joint
- ⅝" by ³⁄₁₆" groove
- Shelf tracks
- Fixed shelf
- ¼" plywood back
- Dado joint
- ³⁄₈" by ³⁄₈" rabbet
- Adjustable shelves
- 1½"
- 2 by 4 kickbase
- Facing
- Dado joint
- Top
- Partition
- **Partition**
- **Hand tool alternatives**
- Butt joints
- Back cut flush with edge
- Drywall screw
- 3d box nail
- Wood plug

Hand tools only? The case shown on the facing page requires a router or table saw to make neat work of rabbets and dadoes. If you're working with hand tools only, don't despair: simply assemble the case with butt joints and then cut the back so it's flush with the outside edges of the unit, as shown in the inset drawing.

CUTTING & ASSEMBLY

Below and on the following page are step-by-step instructions and illustrations for building a typical bookcase.

Cutting. Before you cut, make sure all the stock is the correct thickness and is flat and square.

When you crosscut the top, bottom, fixed shelves, or partitions to length, be sure to add or subtract for the joinery. Cut adjustable shelves 1/16 to 1/8 inch shorter than the space between the uprights.

If you need to rip boards to width, use the same fence setting (for a power saw) or marking gauge setting (for a handsaw) for each board. Remember that if you're recessing the back, the shelves and any interior partitions must be narrower than the top, bottom, and sides.

The back must be square or the finished bookcase will list to the left or right. Check the corners and then measure both diagonals. The measurements should match up.

Joinery. Once the pieces are cut, you can shape any joints. Cut all the rabbets and dadoes with the same depth setting on your router or table saw, being sure to check the settings on scrap lumber first. The fit of a dado should be snug but not too tight; rabbets should fit the mating piece exactly.

If you're recessing shelf tracks, cut the grooves now. Plan to locate the outside edges of both tracks 1½ inches from the front and back edges of the sides and partitions.

Rough-sanding. After cutting and shaping, rough-sand any flaws, lumber stamps, or pencil marks. The more sanding you can do now, the better; it's much easier than waiting until the case is assembled. Be sure not to oversand where the pieces will be joined, or the fit may become too loose.

Gluing up. Every woodworker makes mistakes — the trick is to discover them before you spread the glue. For this rea-

Cutting & Shaping the Pieces

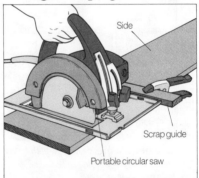

First, crosscut all the boards *to length, making sure to add or subtract for rabbets and dadoes.*

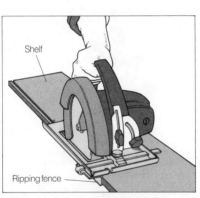

Next, rip shelves and partitions *to width, using the same fence setting for all the cuts.*

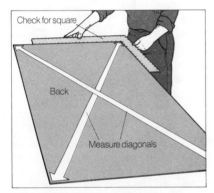

Also cut the back *and check it for square. Corner-to-corner dimensions should be the same.*

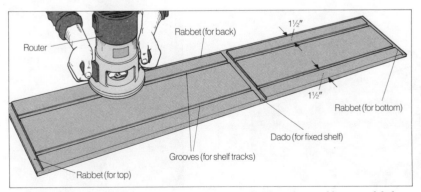

To shape the joints in each side piece, *use a router (as shown) or a table saw and dado head. When laying out the joints, be sure that matching sides "mirror" each other. Top, bottom, and partitions may need shaping, too.*

Rough-sand *the pieces before you assemble them; it's much easier than sanding later. A belt sander is the best tool for the job.*

BUILDING A BOOKCASE

son, dry-fit the case first and make any necessary adjustments.

Everything fits? If the case has no interior partitions, start your assembly by laying one side piece on a flat, smooth surface. Spread glue in all the rabbets and dadoes, using a plumber's flux brush or an ice cream stick; coat the end grain of the matching pieces, too.

If there are any fixed shelves, introduce them into their dadoes first, as shown below, and tap them home with a scrap block and a hammer. If you're recessing the back, be sure to line up the shelf's back edge with the back edge of the rabbet to create a single plane for the back. You can always clean up any minor misalignment in the front later with a plane or belt sander.

Once any fixed shelves are in their dadoes, rotate the assembly onto its front edge, so that the back edge is facing up. Nail or screw each joint. Attach the other side piece; then add the top and bottom.

If there are any partitions, start your assembly by threading them into the dadoes in the top and bottom pieces. Then add the sides.

Attaching the back. Add the back immediately, before the glue dries, and use it to square the case. Simply slip the back into the rabbets or nail one side of the back flush; then rack the case to fit the back, nailing carefully as you go (see drawing at bottom left). Attach the back with a small amount of glue and 3-penny box nails spaced every 4 inches. Once the edges are nailed, snap a chalkline down the center of any fixed shelves or partitions, and nail the back to these as well.

Finishing steps. Scrape off any dried glue, plug or fill holes and dents (see page 42), and do the final sanding. Finish as desired and then install the shelf tracks (see below, at bottom) and the adjustable shelves.

Assembling the Case

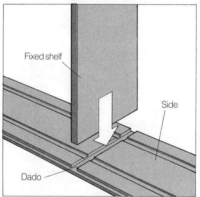

First, thread the ends *of any fixed shelves into the dadoes on one side piece, tapping them home with a scrap block and hammer.*

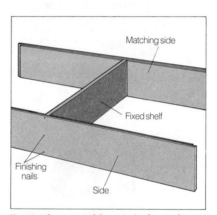

Rotate the assembly *onto its front edge and add the matching side, gluing and nailing or screwing each joint as you go.*

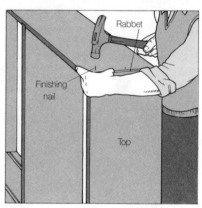

Top and bottom pieces *complete the frame; slip them in the side rabbets and fasten as shown.*

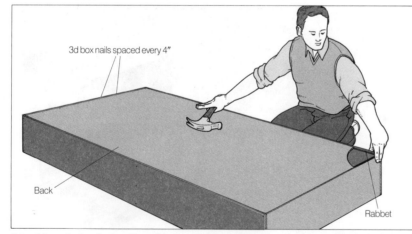

Attaching the back *should square the unit. Rack the case until the back slips down into all the rabbets; then carefully nail it around the edges. Also nail into the back of any fixed shelves or partitions.*

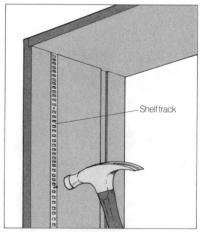

Finally, install shelf tracks: *use a hacksaw to cut tracks to length; secure them with color-matched nails.*

A MODEL OF EFFICIENCY

Strong, clean lines, flush doors, invisible hinges, adjustable shelves, and a crisp white finish all add up to a contemporary European look. Uprights of 1-by solid lumber are faced with 1 by 2s for a sturdier appearance. As shown in the detail photo at left, the cabinet doors on top open to reveal a television, which pulls out on a swiveling shelf; behind the lower doors is a metal-lined compartment for firewood. Architect: Peter Golze.

Cabinets, like the bookcase described on the previous pages, are basically boxes, but in this case fitted with drawers and doors, and sometimes with appliances.

Because they're wide and deep, cabinets are usually made from plywood, which is stronger, more stable, and less expensive than a series of edge-joined solid boards. These plywood boxes, called *carcases,* are then fitted with solid-lumber *faceframes* that hide the exposed plywood edges in front.

Here and on the following pages we present the basics of cabinet design and construction. No matter what your storage or display needs, you can use these guidelines to create a cabinet that fills the bill.

DESIGNING A CABINET

Faceframe cabinets can be divided into two broad categories: *base units,* which sit on the floor, and *wall units,* which are anchored to the wall above floor level. Though they're designed a little differently (see drawings at right and on facing page), both types share the same basic components. Once you're familiar with these components, you'll be able to determine the specific design, dimensions, and joinery for your own cabinets.

The carcase. The carcases of both base and wall cabinets are composed of two ends, a bottom (called a deck), a back, and, in many cases, interior partitions. End panels and decks are normally made from ¾-inch plywood; often, partitions are cut from ⅝-inch plywood and the back from ¼-inch plywood.

A/B fir plywood is sufficient for cabinets you plan to paint, but birch plywood—either shop- or special paint-grade—is better. For stains or a natural finish, choose A-1 or A-2 hardwood panels or vertical-grain fir. Save your best plywood for finished end panels, which will be exposed to view.

Nail rails, made from a 1 by 4 or 1 by 6 and positioned near the top edge of the back, aid in attaching the cabinet to the wall. Most wall units are built with continuous top and bottom rails that fit into notches cut in the partitions and rabbets cut into the ends. Base units typically have only top nail rails, which are fitted between the partitions and end panels and are screwed to the back.

The *kickspace* on a base unit allows you to stand comfortably in front of the cabinet. It should be about 3 inches deep and 4 to 4½ inches high. You can make a kickspace either by notching the end panels and facing this void with a 1-by lumber kickboard or by building a separate base from 2-by material and setting the cabinet (reduced in height) on top during installation. We feature the first method on the following pages; for details on the 2-by base, see pages 48 and 71.

In a large carcase, you'll need top support to square-up the case and hold the partitions vertical. Wall units typically have plywood top panels; base cabinets are fitted with *top braces.* Normally pine 1 by 4s that extend between the end panels at the front and back, top braces also serve as nailers for the countertop. Small vanities sometimes incorporate flat, triangular *corner blocks* (see drawing on facing page) for the same purpose; they're awkward to install, but they leave more room for the sink.

The faceframe. Plywood has one major shortcoming: its unattractive exposed edges. The faceframe, glued and joined into a single "picture frame," is attached to the front of the plywood carcase and hides the edges, presenting a front of solid wood to the world. It also keeps the carcase rigid, facilitates fitting cabinets to walls and other cabinets, and provides jambs for doors and rails for drawer fronts.

Faceframes are composed of rails, stiles, and mullions, all arranged to hide as much end grain as possible. The *rails* run horizontally, the *stiles* are attached vertically to the ends of the rails, and the *mullions* fit between the rails.

Normally, faceframes are made from 1-by hardwood between 1¼ and 4 inches wide. Though the lumber is usually the same species as the plywood used for the carcase, you can choose a contrasting species for accent and then match *it* to the new doors and drawer fronts.

Dimensions. Kitchen cabinets and bathroom vanities are typically built to standard dimensions (see drawing below) to accommodate sinks, manufactured countertops, and appliances. Use these dimensions as a guide to determine the size that best fits your needs.

If you're contemplating a complete set of kitchen or bathroom cabinets, the *Sunset* books *Kitchens* and *Bathrooms* are good places to begin your planning. Your goal—the final step of the design phase—is a set of plan and elevation drawings that detail the number and sizes of drawers and shelf bays. (For information on doors and drawers, see pages 61–69; you won't build these, however, until the carcase and faceframe are completed.)

Standard Dimensions

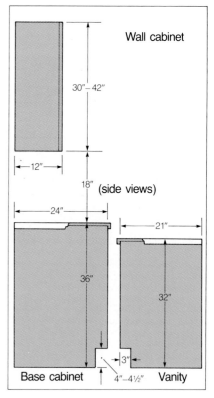

Typical Faceframe Cabinets

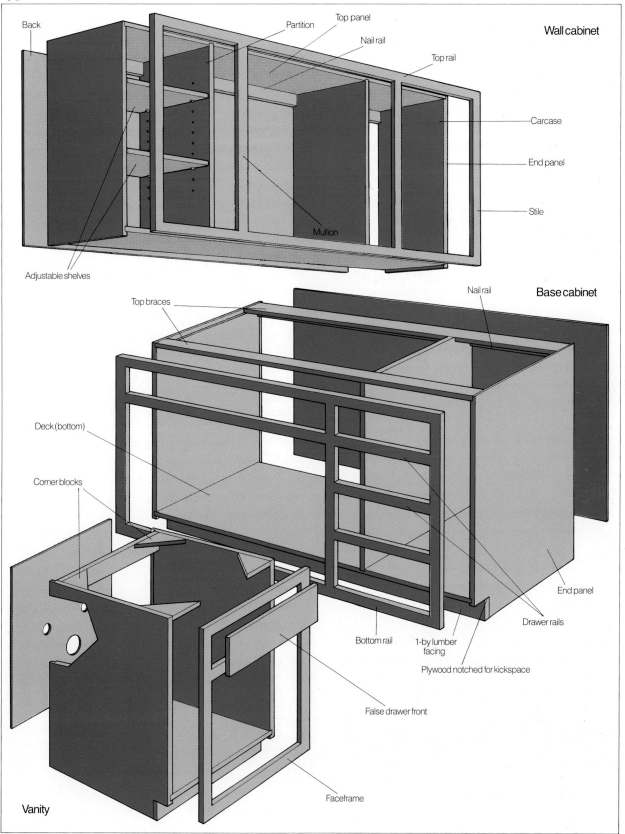

Back

Partition

Top panel

Nail rail

Top rail

Wall cabinet

Carcase

End panel

Stile

Mullion

Adjustable shelves

Nail rail

Base cabinet

Top braces

Deck (bottom)

Corner blocks

End panel

Drawer rails

Bottom rail

1-by lumber facing

Plywood notched for kickspace

False drawer front

Faceframe

Vanity

CULINARY CRAFTSMANSHIP

Solid oak envelops this kitchen with its richly grained warmth. Creating a vertical motif, frame-and-panel doors are assembled from edge-glued strips of solid lumber. Drawer fronts, faceframe, and countertop trim are matching lumber. As shown at right, 1-by shelves are lipped for more secure storage; brackets and a ledger support the shelves. Design: Richard White.

BASIC CABINETRY

If your plans include long stretches of cabinetry, you'll probably have to build them in sections. Natural breaks occur at corners, walls, and freestanding appliances, but every partition gives you an opportunity to break.

When you're thinking about construction, don't forget to take into account the size of your work area and the route from shop to installation point. One compromise is to build smaller units and connect them later on with one faceframe and a continuous countertop.

Joinery options. Basic carcase joints, with variations for both hand and power tools, are shown in the drawing at right.

If you're working with a table saw or router, plan to join the deck, end panels, and any partitions with dado joints or the even stronger rabbet-and-dado joints (see page 37). The top braces sit atop rabbets in each end panel. Also notch each partition for the top braces.

Working with hand tools only? You can still build a first-rate case — just use basic butt joints, ledgers, and screws for reinforcement, as shown.

By insetting the cabinet back, you not only hide it on a finished end, but you can also create a scribe allowance (see below) at the same time. Cut rabbets in the end panels. Or, if you're limited to hand tools, cut the back to fit inside the case; then fasten it to small cleats or molding.

The parts of the faceframe must be connected with more strength than a simple butt joint can offer; blind-doweling (see page 36) is the answer.

Scribe allowance. Wherever the end of a cabinet butts a wall or another cabinet, the carcase itself should be built ½ inch short. The resulting gap is covered by the faceframe; when the cabinet is installed, the edge of the stile that projects beyond the carcase — the *scribe allowance* — is sanded or planed to fit the space exactly (see page 71).

You'll also need to provide for a scribe allowance at the back edge of plywood end panels where they meet

Joinery Options

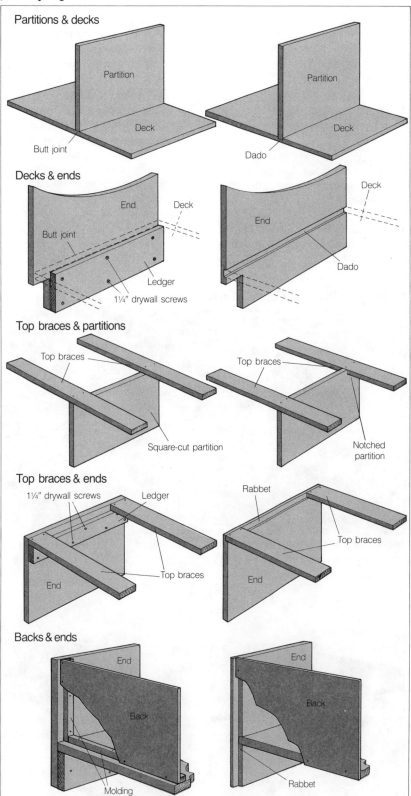

To join the components of the plywood carcase, *choose either the simple, efficient joints on the left, easily made with hand tools, or the more sophisticated options on the right.*

BASIC CABINETRY

a wall. The simplest way to do this is to deepen the rabbet that the back fits into—make the rabbet ½ inch deep for a ¼-inch plywood back.

CUTTING & ASSEMBLING THE CARCASE

Building plywood cabinets requires attention to accuracy. And given the size and scope of the project, the job also demands physical dexterity.

Cutting the pieces. Make a rough drawing of each component—back, deck, end panels, partitions, and shelves. Carefully mark the dimensions of each piece and any dadoes or rabbets. Plywood grain usually runs vertically on end panels or partitions, and from end to end on decks and shelves.

A table saw is the most accurate tool for cutting carcase parts, but even pros sometimes use another saw to first divide up plywood sheets into more manageable pieces. Whatever tool you're using, it's easiest to rip the plywood to a given width and then crosscut pieces to length. Also cut the top braces and nail rails.

Next, cut any joints. If you're working with a table saw or router, rabbet the end panels for the top braces (base units only), nail rails (wall units only), and back. If you're dadoing the end panels to receive the deck and any fixed shelves, or if you're dadoing the deck to receive partitions, cut these joints as well.

If you're cutting with hand tools, screw ledgers for the deck and top braces, and cleats or molding for the back, to the end panels.

The last steps before assembly are notching the end panels for the kickspace, notching partitions for the nail rails, and drilling peg holes for any adjustable shelves. A predrilled template, shown at the bottom of the page, is a big help for aligning the holes.

Cutting & Shaping Carcase Parts

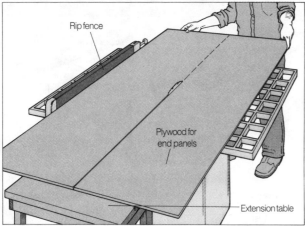

To begin, rip the plywood to width. *A table saw equipped with an extension table ensures clean cuts.*

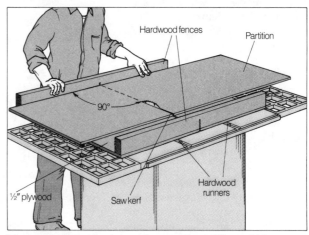

Next, crosscut each piece. *A homemade cutoff box, which runs in the miter gauge slots, helps guide crosscuts.*

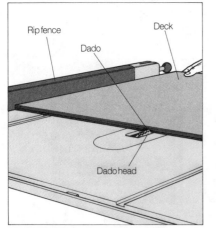

Shape joints *in the deck, panel ends, and partitions as needed with a table saw (as shown) or with an electric router.*

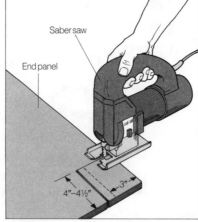

Notch end panels *for the kickspace, making sure to leave an extra ¾ inch for the 1-by lumber facing you'll add.*

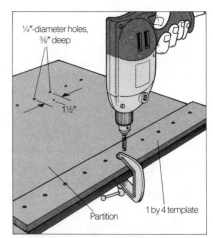

Drill shelf peg holes *before assembly. A predrilled template helps keep hole spacing consistent from row to row.*

Assembling the carcase. Build the carcase from the inside out and from the bottom up. Glue all connections and secure them with 2-inch drywall screws in areas that won't show and 6-penny finishing nails in exposed areas.

Working on a flat, level surface, tilt the deck up on its front edge; then glue and screw the partitions to the deck. If you're butt-joining the deck and partitions, you may need some assistance — since the glue is slippery, it's very tough to hold the partition on the layout lines while you're driving screws from below. For help, temporarily nail cleats to the deck top along the layout lines.

Now add the end panels, working quickly before the glue dries. Secure the connections with drywall screws or with finishing nails.

Next, attach the top of the case. Mark the top braces or top panel for partition locations by holding them down at deck level where the partitions are already fastened. This will ensure that the partitions are plumb and parallel to the end panels.

On base units, drive two 2-inch drywall screws through the wall end into the end of each top brace, and two down from the top into the ledger or rabbet on the finished end. Fasten the top panel of a wall unit in the same manner as the deck. Then drive dry-wall screws down through the top brace or top panel into each partition at both the front and back (see drawing at bottom left).

If your partitions are notched for the nail rails and/or the ends are rabbeted, screw the nail rails in place now. (On base units, you can wait until the back is installed.)

Spread glue sparingly around the rabbeted back edge of the carcase and set the back in place. Using the fit of the back as a guide, rack the carcase as necessary. Secure the back with 3-penny box nails every 4 inches, starting at a top corner. Then nail through the back into the deck and finish off by nailing into the top brace and partitions.

Putting the Box Together

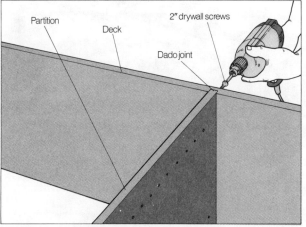

First, join any partitions to the deck, using glue and screws driven through the deck from below.

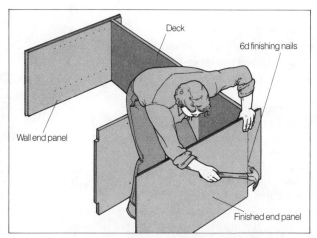

Attach the end panels to the deck. Secure the joints with screws where they won't show; in exposed areas, use finishing nails.

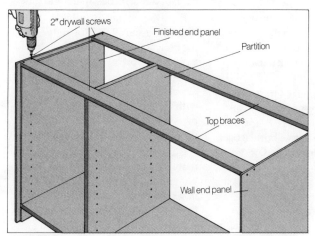

Add the top braces, screwing through a wall end panel or down into a rabbet or ledger on a finished end. Also drive screws into each partition.

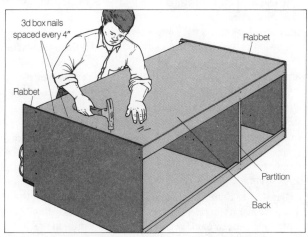

To complete the carcase, spread glue sparingly in the rabbets and along the deck, top brace, and partitions; then rack the case to fit the back and nail the back in place.

BASIC CABINETRY

If you're assembling a base cabinet, nail 1-by facing to the kick-space notches on the end panels.

ADDING THE FACEFRAME

Cutting and assembling the faceframe takes patience and attention to detail: the joints must be tight and the frame must be square.

Cutting. A neat job starts at the layout phase. Measure your completed carcase carefully and tailor the faceframe to it, adding a ½-inch scribe allowance at wall ends. On finished ends, make sure that the faceframe will sit slightly proud of the plywood face. (The excess can be planed or sanded off later.) Plan to align the top of the bottom rail so it's flush with the deck.

After ripping your stock to width, mark the best face on each piece; be sure to crosscut the correct side to minimize splintering.

Once you've cut all the pieces, drill them out for dowels. You'll need ⅜-inch-diameter, 2-inch-long fluted dowels. Use two dowels for 2-inch or wider rails and mullions, and one dowel for narrower pieces. Drill the holes about 1/16 inch long to allow space in the bottom for excess glue. Make sure all the pieces index correctly by mocking them up before you glue.

Gluing and clamping. Gluing and clamping a large faceframe can be something of a juggling act: it's important to keep a logical order and to move quickly. Work from the inside out—mullions and drawer rails first, followed by top and bottom rails and stiles.

Spread glue on the surfaces to be joined; then coat the dowels with glue and insert them in the holes of one piece (they should enter the holes with finger pressure). Immediately assemble the other piece and clamp the joint.

The key to clamping the frame is to keep it flat and square. Lay the frame atop long pipe or bar clamps that sit on a level floor or flat table (see drawing at top of page); these clamps should support the frame along its length. Posi-

Faceframes: The Final Step

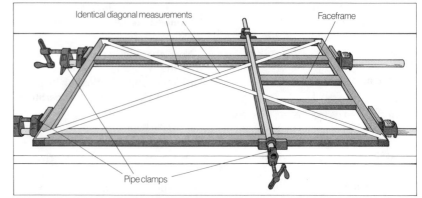

To make sure the faceframe is flat and square, *keep it down on long pipe clamps and measure the diagonals—they should be the same.*

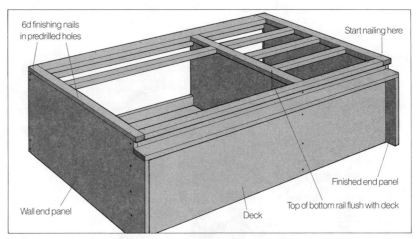

Nail the faceframe *to the carcase, starting at the bottom of a finished end. Nail that stile, then the bottom rail, and up the opposite stile. Finally, nail through the top rail and any mullions.*

tion shorter clamps perpendicular to the others to hold the mullions tight to the top and bottom rails.

Measure the diagonals of the frame before you cinch down on the clamps. If the frame is out of square by 1/16 inch or more, you'll have to rack it using a pipe clamp on an angle.

Make sure the frame is sitting right down on the bar or pipe of the lower clamps. If a rail begins to bow upward in the middle of the frame, bring it back down with a C-clamp hooked under the clamp beneath.

Attaching the faceframe. On the finest cabinets, the faceframe has no puttied nail holes—only glue is used to connect it to the carcase. But this procedure takes a good deal of experience and requires a lot of clamps. It's more

practical to use a combination of nails (6-penny finishing nails in predrilled holes about 12 inches apart) and glue.

Place the cabinet on its back. Spread glue on all the front edges of the plywood and then carefully lay the faceframe in place, making sure it overhangs the finished end panel slightly. Check that the top of the deck is flush with the top of the bottom rail. Drill a pilot hole at the bottom corner of a finished end and drive the nail.

Continue up this stile, making sure that there are no gaps between the plywood and hardwood and that the faceframe slightly overhangs the end. Don't hesitate to clamp between nails if you see any gaps. Finish nailing as shown above. Then set all nails, fill the holes, and sand lightly before finishing.

BLEACHED BIRCH

Bright white tiles and drawer pulls accent the cool elegance of these bleached birch kitchen cabinets. Though constructed separately, when installed they look like a single built-in unit. Custom setup includes leaded glass doors and compartments for the ovens and refrigerator. As shown at left, gracefully shaped drawer fronts match the frames on the frame-and-panel doors. Design: Nancy Cowall Cutler and Ruth Soforenko Associates.

A LOOK AT EUROPEAN-STYLE CABINETS

A fresh cabinet style, featuring uninterrupted stretches of doors and drawer fronts and concealed hardware, is showing up in new homes and remodels. Called European cabinets, they offer several advantages over traditional faceframe units: a trim appearance, more usable interior space, and, best of all for the do-it-yourselfer, no blind-doweling or faceframe clamping. For examples of European cabinets, see the photos on pages 43 and 51. Here's a look at their parts.

The basic box

The carcase for a European cabinet is quite simple: it's basically a ¾-inch plywood box with a ¼-inch plywood back attached. Thin strips of hardwood banding cover the exposed plywood edges. Rabbet-and-dado joints (see page 37) are best for carcase connections; mitered corners give the banding a neat look. To simplify assembly and installation, the boxes are usually placed on a separate kickbase.

Doors & drawers

Overlay doors and drawer fronts create the "one-piece" look, with only a slight gap—⅛ inch or so—between components. Both doors and drawer fronts are typically flat panels—either A-1 or A-2 lumber-core plywood, or a lesser plywood grade or other sheet product covered with plastic laminate or wood veneer. Mitered edge banding that matches the carcase front covers panel edges.

Invisible hinges

These imported hinges are the key to the European style. They come in two pieces: one is fastened to the inside of the carcase; the other is housed in a round mortise—typically 1⅜-inch diameter—drilled in the door. The drilling requires a Forstner bit, a portable drill press, and a bit of care. But once installed, the hinges are easy to adjust, allowing you to fine-tune the doors up, down, in, or out for an exact fit.

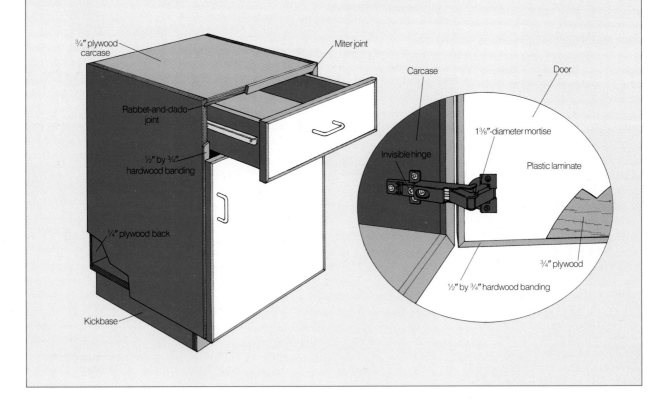

¾" plywood carcase

Miter joint

Rabbet-and-dado joint

½" by ¾" hardwood banding

¼" plywood back

Kickbase

Carcase

Door

1⅜"-diameter mortise

Plastic laminate

Invisible hinge

¾" plywood

½" by ¾" hardwood banding

Doors

Study any cabinet door and you'll most likely find it's made either from plywood, in which case it's called a *flat* door, or from a panel surrounded by a frame, called *frame-and-panel* construction.

You'll also notice that there are several ways to mount a door with respect to the cabinet face. A *flush* door is mounted inside the opening, with its face flush with the front of the cabinet or faceframe. On a *lipped* door, a rabbet is cut around the inside edges of the door so that half its thickness projects beyond the front or faceframe. An *overlay* door overlaps the edges of the opening and is mounted with its inside face against the faceframe. Either flat or frame-and-panel doors can also serve as *sliding* doors, which move back and forth on tracks.

Designing Doors

When designing your doors, first decide whether they'll be flat or frame-and-panel; then choose their front style — flush, lipped, or overlay. Here's how to determine their size and material.

Dimensions. The size of any door — flush, lipped, overlay, or sliding — depends on the exact size of the opening, and, in some cases, on the mounting hardware you choose (see page 65).

To determine the size, first accurately measure the height and width of the opening. Make a flush door the exact size of the opening; you'll need to plane or sand it to fit later. A lipped door should overlap the front ¼ inch all around, so add ½ inch total to the length and width. (One exception: Double doors are not rabbeted where they meet, so don't add for rabbets along these edges.)

Overlay doors can overlap the opening as much as you like — just be sure they won't interfere with other doors or drawer fronts. (A ¼-inch overlap is sufficient.) Because the back edges of these doors are often back-beveled or undercut in some other way, you'll

have to add extra for these edge treatments.

To determine the width of each of a pair of sliding doors, divide the width of the opening in half and add half the amount of the overlap when closed — a 1-inch overlap is typical. To determine the height, subtract the allowance for the tracks (as specified by the manufacturer) from the height of the opening.

Door materials. Though you can make a flat door by edge-gluing solid boards together, it's much easier to use sheet products, such as plywood. In a frame-and-panel door, the frame pieces are made from solid stock and the panel from plywood or solid lumber.

Except for the panels in frame-and-panel doors, which should be ¼ to ½ inch thick depending on the style,

¾-inch plywood or 1-by or ¼ lumber is your best bet. A/B fir plywood is sufficient for flat doors if you plan to paint, but birch plywood — either shop- or special paint-grade — is better. For stains or a natural finish, lumber-core hardwood plywood is tops.

Rails and stiles for frame-and-panel doors are often red oak or birch, though many other hardwood species as well as vertical-grain fir are used. Sliding doors are typically ¼-inch hardboard or plate glass, or ¾-inch plywood.

Flat Plywood Doors

A flat plywood door is the simplest type to make, whether it's flush, lipped, overlay, or sliding. Plywood is highly resistant to warping, and, unlike solid-lumber doors, you don't

Basic Door Types

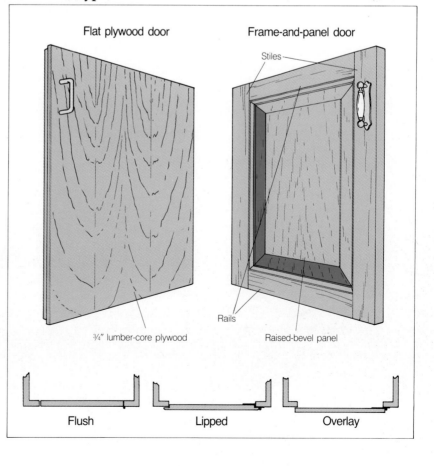

Flat plywood door

¾" lumber-core plywood

Frame-and-panel door

Stiles

Rails

Raised-bevel panel

Flush   Lipped   Overlay

MUSIC LIBRARY

From Vivaldi on tape to violins on display, the contents of this wall system are mostly musical. At left, a vertical row of open shelves organizes sheet music for easy access. Standard bookshelves accommodate stereo components, as well as records and books. As shown at right, bifold doors of classical frame-and-panel design open to reveal a cavernous compartment for a cello. Design: John Kolkka.

have to cut and fit several pieces of wood together.

To create a uniform appearance, it's best to lay out adjacent doors and drawer fronts on the same panel and cut them all at once. The grain typically runs vertically.

Cutting procedures and edge treatments for plywood doors vary, depending on whether they're flush, lipped, or overlay, and whether you plan a natural, stained, or opaque finish.

■ *Flush doors* are typically cut the exact size of the opening, with a back-bevel of 1° to 2° on the latch side. If you opt for solid-lumber banding to cover plywood edges, be sure to cut your doors shorter in height and width. Glue the strips to the edges; "clamp" them with masking tape.

■ *Lipped doors* must be rabbeted on the back. Cut ⅜- by ⅜-inch rabbets on all edges unless they're double doors. In this case, cut both doors as one panel, rabbet the edges, and then rip the door down the center to divide it in half.

Lipped plywood doors intended for a natural or stained finish aren't usually shaped on the front edges because the plywood veneers show up. If you're planning to paint, though, you can round-over these edges with a router and ¼-inch rounding-over bit or chamfering bit. Fill any veneer voids carefully; then sand.

Frame-and-Panel Doors: Some Options

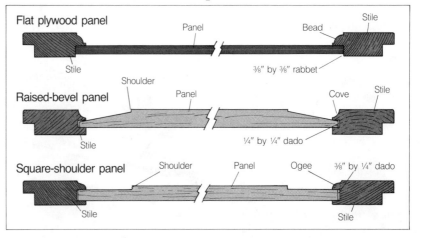

■ *Overlay doors* can either be cut to size with squared edges or cut oversize and then back-beveled about 30°; the back-bevel allows you to hide veneers without banding and serves as a finger pull. For best results, cut the bevels on a table saw and round off sharp edges.

FRAME-AND-PANEL CONSTRUCTION

Frame-and-panel designs break down into three basic panel types: flat, raised-bevel, and square-shoulder. All three types are illustrated in the drawing at the top of the page. Plywood panels can be secured to the frame in either rabbets or dadoes; solid-wood panels must be housed in dadoes to allow for movement.

Making the frame. To connect the stiles and rails that form the frame, you can use blind-doweled butt joints, end-laps, open mortise and tenons, or blind mortise and tenons.

If you're joining the panel to the frame with dadoes, cut them at the same time you make the stiles and rails, stopping them short of the areas to be joined. For a raised-bevel panel, cut the dadoes ¼ inch wide and ¼ inch deep; for a square-shoulder design, make them ⅜ by ¼ inch.

If you're planning to use rabbets to affix the panel to the frame, assemble the frame first; then cut the rabbets for the panel.

At this point, you can also shape the inside edges of the frame by dry-clamping the frame and using a router and appropriate bit.

Plywood Door Edge Treatments

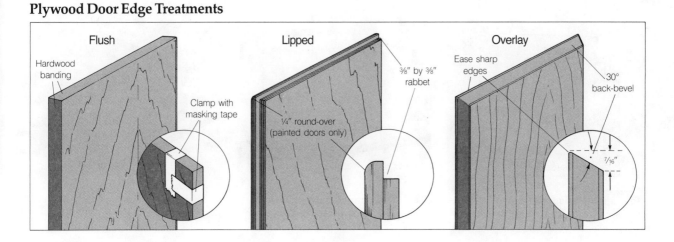

Doors

Cutting the panel. Below are instructions for cutting flat, raised-bevel, and square-shoulder panels.

■ *A flat panel* is easy to make from ¼-inch plywood, and you won't have to worry about wood movement. Cut the panel to fit the space plus the width of the rabbets or dadoes.

■ *A raised-bevel panel* can be made from either ½-inch lumber-core plywood or ½-inch solid stock (a must for a natural finish). Make solid panels less than 6 inches wide from a single piece of wood. Wider than that, select and edge-glue narrower pieces to minimize warping.

When cutting a panel to fit into dadoes, be sure to measure the bottom-to-bottom distance between the dadoes first. Cut the panel short—⅛ inch for plywood, ³⁄₁₆ to ¼ inch for solid lumber—in length and width to allow the panel to "float."

You can cut raised bevels with a table saw, radial-arm saw, or router, but the table saw is the tool of choice. For a ½-inch panel, raise the saw's blade to 1¼ inches and set the rip fence ³⁄₁₆ inch away from the blade; tilt the blade 10° away from the fence. Make the bevel cuts, as shown at the top of the page. To square-cut the shoulder, return the blade to vertical and adjust the blade height and fence; make a second series of cuts.

Cutting Panels with a Table Saw

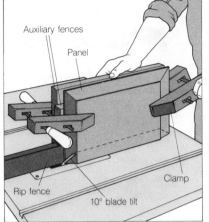

A raised-bevel panel *is simplest to cut on a table saw; a jig makes the cuts safer and more accurate.*

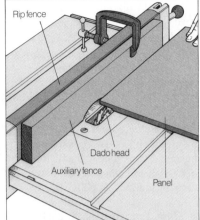

Form a square shoulder *in successive passes, like a wide rabbet. An auxiliary fence protects the rip fence.*

■ *To make a square-shoulder panel,* use either a table saw and dado head (see above, at right) or a router and straight bit. Set the blade height or bit depth for ⅛ inch. Make the first cut so the shoulder is 1¼ inches from the edge; then finish the rabbet with successive passes.

Assembling the door. To assemble your door, first join one stile to the two rails, using glue (and dowels, if required). If you're inserting a panel into dadoes, slide it into place now. (Note: To avoid gluing the panel to the frame, round off the corners of the panel slightly and coat the edges with

paste wax before inserting it.) Then glue up the other stile.

Clamp the assembly, using two bar or pipe clamps, one centered under each rail. Be sure the clamps lie on a flat surface; otherwise, the door will wind up twisted.

If you're attaching a flat plywood panel to rabbets, wait until the frame has dried; then cut ⅜- by ⅜-inch rabbets on the back of the frame. Apply glue sparingly, set the panel in place, and secure it with brads or clamps.

Finishing touches. If you're constructing a lipped door, cut the ⅜- by

Assembling Frame-and-Panel Doors

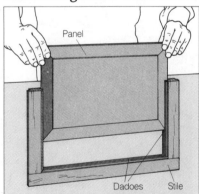

To assemble a dadoed frame, *join rails to one stile, slide the panel into the dadoes, and add the remaining stile.*

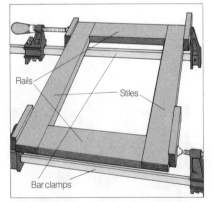

Clamp the completed frame, *with or without the panel in place, using one bar or pipe clamp under each rail.*

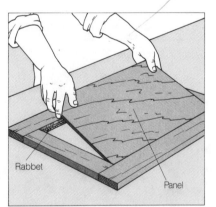

A flat plywood panel *requires glue to hold it in place. Press the panel into the rabbets; secure it with brads or clamps.*

⅜-inch rabbets in the frame's outside edges for the lip. Also, you may wish to round-over the front edges with a router and ¼-inch rounding-over bit.

An overlay door may need a 30° back-bevel (as shown on page 63) or another decorative edge treatment. A flush door should be back-beveled 1° to 2° on the latch side.

Finally, sand your door to prepare it for a fine finish.

HANGING YOUR DOORS

Shown at right is a sampling of the array of hinges and other hardware available to hang flush, lipped, and overlay doors, as well as two ways to mount sliding doors. Whenever possible, opt for self-closing hinges, which don't require a separate catch to keep them closed. If you do need catches, magnetic types are best — they're less dependent on strict alignment and don't wear out.

Decorative butt and semiconcealed hinges are straightforward to install, but other types may require some careful mortising or drilling. To shape a rectangular mortise, use either a chisel or an electric router and template. (You'll still need a chisel to square-up router-cut corners.)

Typically, the door-hanging sequence proceeds as follows: (1) fasten the hinges on the door; (2) line up the door and mark the upper screw holes on the faceframe or carcase; (3) install the top screws; (4) if the swing and alignment check out, install the remaining screws.

For flush or lipped doors, first be sure the carcase is upright, plumb, and level. Plane a flush door to fit the opening; then even out the spacing all around with paper strips or thin shims. When you're hanging a lipped door, try setting it on a pair of nickels (one in each lower corner). You can mount overlay doors with the unit on its back, but be sure to recheck the alignment once the cabinet is installed.

Door knobs and pulls, available in great profusion, usually screw on, though some may bolt through the door or drawer front. Flush knobs (designed for sliding doors) and pulls must be mounted in holes or mortises.

Door Hinge Details

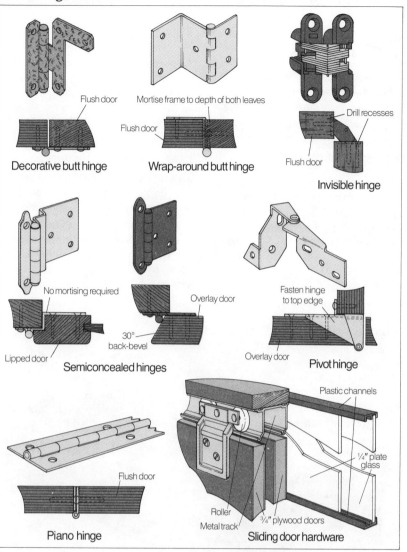

Decorative butt hinge
Flush door
Wrap-around butt hinge
Mortise frame to depth of both leaves
Flush door
Invisible hinge
Drill recesses
Flush door

No mortising required
Lipped door
Semiconcealed hinges
30° back-bevel
Overlay door
Fasten hinge to top edge
Overlay door
Pivot hinge

Plastic channels
¼" plate glass
Roller
Metal track
¾" plywood doors
Sliding door hardware

Flush door
Piano hinge

Door Catches

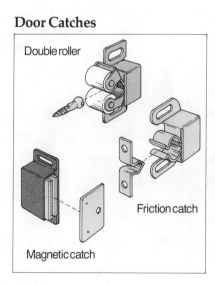

Double roller
Friction catch
Magnetic catch

Chiseling a Mortise

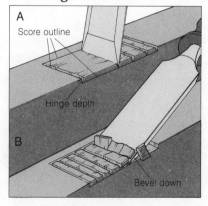

A
Score outline
Hinge depth
B
Bevel down

To mortise by hand, *first make parallel chisel cuts (A); then chip out waste wood with the chisel bevel side down (B).*

DRAWERS

First-rate drawer design and assembly present a challenge for even the seasoned woodworker. Not only must you size, cut, and join five or six pieces of wood, but you also need to fit the drawer precisely into a cabinet recess.

Drawers come in three basic styles: flush, lipped, or overlay. A *flush* drawer lines up even with the front of the cabinet or faceframe. On a *lipped* drawer, a rabbet is cut around the inside edges of the front so that half its thickness projects beyond the front or faceframe. The entire front of an *overlay* drawer sits outside the faceframe. Materials and joinery for all three types can be varied to suit your budget and skill level.

DESIGNING DRAWERS

Before cutting and assembling your drawers, you'll need to choose your materials and joinery, and figure the sizes exactly.

Materials. Drawer fronts can be either solid lumber or plywood. Red oak, birch, and fir—1-by or 4/4 thickness—are the most popular solid-lumber species. If you opt for plywood, choose lumber-core panels for best results.

If the door style is frame-and-panel, drawer fronts are typically made from solid lumber of the same species as the door's frame. If you're using plywood, plan to cut both drawer fronts and

doors from the same sheet, with the grain running in the same direction for all pieces.

Baltic birch plywood, ½ inch thick, is tops for sides and backs. Solid pine is also widely used, though it's not as strong or stable as plywood. Drawer bottoms are typically ¼-inch A/C fir plywood or hardboard, but hardwood plywood adds a nice touch.

Joinery options. Drawers are strongest if the back, sides, and bottom are joined with dadoes and rabbets, but simple butt joints will work, too.

Front and side components and their connections depend on whether you're building flush, lipped, or overlay drawers. It's easier to build flush and overlay drawers with a *false front*, as shown; even lipped drawers are sometimes put together this way. This method allows you to construct the basic box as a single unit, hang it, and then align the decorative front exactly.

Dimensions. Start with the box height: unless you're using bottom runners to hang the drawer (see page 69), make the height the same as the opening minus ¼ inch. Drawer width is also nominally the opening minus ¼ inch, but you'll have to subtract extra for any side guides—most require ½-inch clearance on each side.

As a general rule, make the drawer ¼ inch less than the depth of the recess, unless your guides require additional space in back. Be sure to allow for your front style: measure flush drawers from the front edge of the faceframe, add ⅜ inch for lipped drawers, and add ¾ inch for overlay drawers.

Next, size the decorative front. A flush front should fit the opening snugly: make its dimensions the exact size of the opening (you'll plane it later on). Lipped front edges are rabbeted so that ¼ inch projects beyond the opening on all sides; make both the height and width of the front ½ inch more than your opening. Overlay fronts also overhang the faceframe ¼ inch, but if you plan to back-bevel the edges (see page 68), you'll need to add ½ inch extra on all sides.

Anatomy of a Drawer

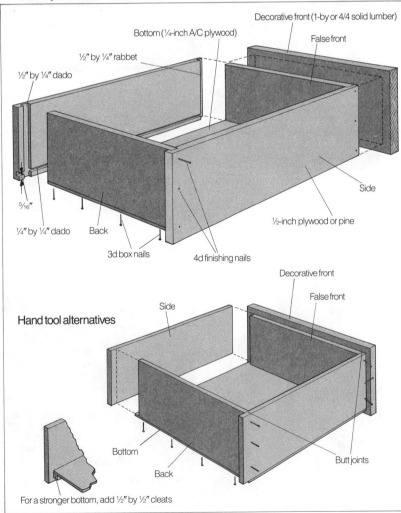

Decorative front (1-by or 4/4 solid lumber)

False front

Bottom (¼-inch A/C plywood)

½" by ¼" rabbet

½" by ¼" dado

Side

½-inch plywood or pine

⁵⁄₁₆"

¼" by ¼" dado   Back

3d box nails   4d finishing nails

Hand tool alternatives

Side

Decorative front

False front

Bottom

Back

Butt joints

For a stronger bottom, add ½" by ½" cleats

Drawer Front Details: Flush & Lipped Drawers

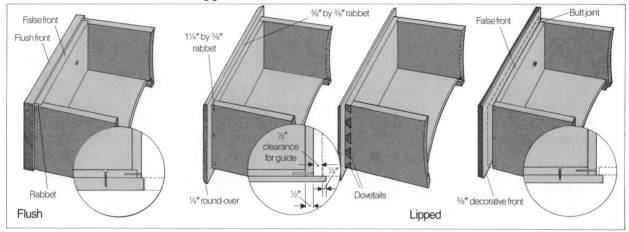

Flush

- False front
- Flush front
- Rabbet
- ⅜" by ⅜" rabbet
- 1¼" by ⅜" rabbet
- ½" clearance for guide
- ¼"
- ½"
- ¼" round-over
- Dovetails

Lipped

- False front
- Butt joint
- ⅜" decorative front

CUTTING & ASSEMBLY

Once the drawers are designed, you're ready to cut and assemble them.

Cutting. Rip stock for the sides, back, and false front (if you're using one) to width. Next, crosscut the parts to length, being sure to add or subtract any extra for joinery.

If you're joining the box parts with rabbets and dadoes, cut them now. In each side piece, cut dadoes for the back and bottom, and rabbets for the false front; also dado the false front for the bottom. You can cut these joints with a table saw and dado head or with a router and straight bit. A homemade router table, like the one shown below, makes routing narrow drawer parts much simpler.

If your drawer's bottom will sit inside dadoes, cut it 1⁄16 inch shorter than the distance to the bottom of the dado on each side and on the front to allow the piece to expand and contract. If you're building the butt-joined version, size the bottom to the box's outside dimensions; if it will sit on cleats, size it to fit inside the box.

Cut the decorative front, cut front-to-side joints as necessary, and shape the edges as described below.

■ *Flush drawer fronts* don't require any joinery if you've used a false front. For a tighter fit, back-bevel the edges slightly — about 1° to 2°.

■ *A lipped front* can be joined to the sides with either rabbets or dovetails, unless you've used a false front. If you choose rabbets, you'll want to end up with a ⅜- by ⅜-inch rabbet around all four inside edges to form the lip. To accommodate the sides, cut the side rabbets an extra ½ inch wide — or ⅞ inch total. And if you're using side guides, add to the rabbet widths again: make them each 1¼ inches wide for a ½-inch guide thickness.

Hand tool users can simulate a lipped drawer with false front construction: just add a decorative front of ⅜-inch material, as shown above.

To shape dovetails, use a router and dovetail fixture (see drawing below). Cut the dovetails for one corner in the

Two Router Shortcuts

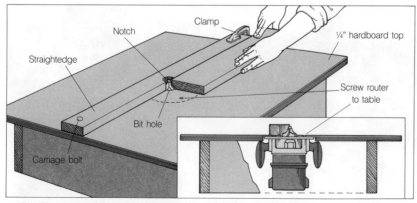

- Notch
- Clamp
- Straightedge
- ¼" hardboard top
- Bit hole
- Screw router to table
- Carriage bolt

A simple router table *makes drawer joinery and edge-shaping a breeze. Just mount your router upside-down beneath a flat tabletop, as shown in the inset. The fence, a hardwood straightedge, guides the work past the bit.*

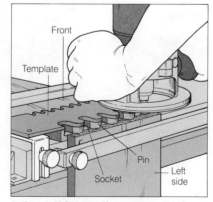

- Front
- Template
- Pin
- Socket
- Left side

A dovetail fixture *allows you to rout the pins in one drawer piece and the sockets in the other at the same time.*

DRAWERS

front and one side. Remove the side piece and reposition the template to cut the dovetail sockets in the front ⅜ or ⅞ inch longer, depending on whether or not you're using side guides. Repeat this process for the other front corner. Then cut a ⅜-inch-wide by ⅜-inch-deep rabbet on all four edges of the inside face (with side guides, make the side rabbets ⅞ inch wide).

Cut the dado for the bottom ⁵⁄₁₆ inch above the bottom lip. If you're dovetailing, stop the dado ¼ inch short of both lips.

The front edges of solid-lumber lipped fronts are typically rounded over with a router and ¼-inch rounding-over bit.

■ *Overlay drawer fronts* can have a wide assortment of edge treatments (see drawing at top of page). You can rout any number of edge shapes in solid lumber. With plywood, opt for either edge-banding or — if you're armed with a table saw — the popular 30° back-bevel. The back-bevel not only hides plywood edges but also provides a finger grip for opening the drawer. Cut this front oversize; then go back and cut the bevels.

Assembly. Before you glue, take the time to dry-fit the drawer carefully and check it for square.

Begin the assembly with the back-to-side joints (if you're dovetailing,

Drawer Front Details: Overlay Drawers

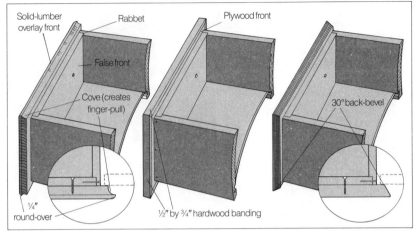

start with the front-to-side joints). Spread glue inside any dadoes and along the end grain of the back. Position the pieces and secure each joint with three 4-penny finishing nails.

Next, add the false front or, in the case of a lipped drawer, the actual front. Again, use glue and finishing nails to make the connections, unless you're joining dovetails; in that case, glue alone is sufficient.

To install a butt-joined bottom, simply flip the box upside down, square the edges to the bottom, and nail it on with 3-penny box nails spaced every few inches. Or, if you're using cleats, nail them to the inside of the box and then nail the bottom to the cleats.

If the bottom fits in dadoes, slide it in until it's flush with the back. Check

for square with a try or combination square and by measuring the corner-to-corner diagonals. If the box is out of square, pull it into line with bar or pipe clamps; or rack it by pushing firmly on the long diagonal. Then nail the bottom to the back with 3-penny box nails.

Once the basic box is together, round-over the top edges of the sides and the back edge of the false front, as shown in the drawing below. Finish-sand the pieces and seal the inside with shellac, sanding sealer, or wax.

INSTALLING YOUR DRAWERS

When it's time to mount your drawers, you can choose between traditional

Assembling the Box

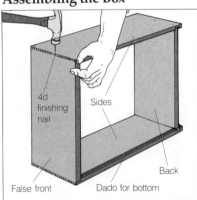

Begin assembly *by gluing and nailing the sides and back together; then add the false front or the actual front.*

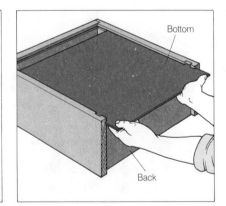

Slide in the bottom *(if it's dadoed), square-up the assembly, and nail the bottom to the back.*

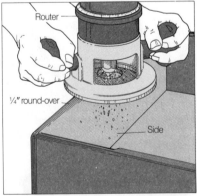

For a finished look, *round-over the edges of the sides and the back edge of the false front with a router or file.*

wooden runners and manufactured metal guide systems.

Wooden runners. The simplest way to support a drawer is on wooden side runners (see drawing at right). Hardwood strips, typically ½ by ¾ inch, are screwed to the sides of the carcase; the matching grooves in the drawer sides should be about ¹⁄₁₆ inch wider and deeper. Elongated screw holes allow the runners to expand and contract. A coat of wax helps cut friction.

Very wide or heavy drawers require a center runner. In this case, a grooved wooden or plastic track is fastened to the drawer bottom; the runner sits on a dust panel (shelf) dadoed into the carcase sides.

Manufactured guides. For the smoothest, most trouble-free drawer action, choose prefabricated metal ball-bearing guide sets attached to the drawer bottom or sides. Bottom guides are sufficient for many applications, but side guides handle more weight and operate more smoothly. Bottom guides typically require ³⁄₁₆-inch clearance top and bottom and ⅛ inch on each side, and side guides ½ inch on both sides, but check the manufacturer's instructions to be sure.

If your opening includes an overhanging faceframe and you're using side guides, you'll need to bring the mounting surface flush with the edge with filler strips.

Before installing the drawers, be sure your carcase is plumb, level, and untwisted. Find the elongated screw holes on the guides and mark their centers with a scratch awl. Install only these screws. Try the drawer out; for fine adjustments, loosen the screws slightly and reposition the hardware in the slots. Once all is aligned, remove the drawer and drive the remaining screws.

Adding the decorative front. Fasten the decorative front (if there is one) from inside with 1-inch screws. To make alignment easier, you can first drill oversize pilot holes in the false front and then use screws and small flat washers to attach the decorative front. To adjust it, just loosen the screws a bit and move the front where you want it.

Drawer Guide Options

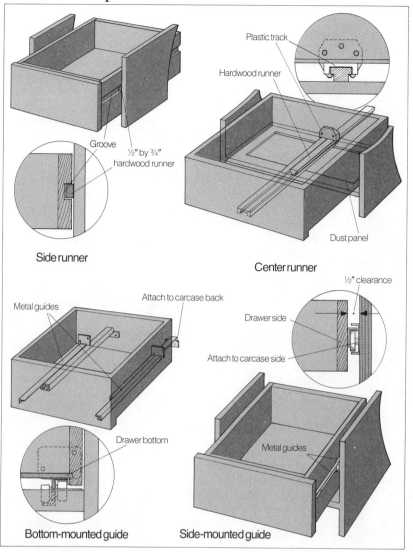

Side runner

Center runner

Bottom-mounted guide

Side-mounted guide

Mounting Drawers: Two Tips

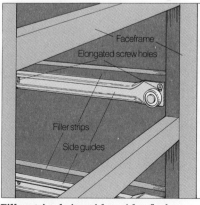

Filler strips bring side guides *flush with the faceframe. Drive screws through elongated holes and then align.*

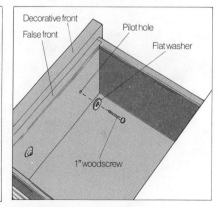

To install a decorative front, *screw through the false front. Oversize pilot holes and small flat washers allow for adjustment.*

INSTALLING YOUR PROJECT

No project is finished until it's installed. Simple bookshelves may require only brackets or other hardware anchored to the wall or ceiling. Installing a heavy bookcase or a new bank of cabinets calls for some extra steps.

FASTENING TO WALLS & CEILINGS

Most house walls and ceilings are not solid; rather, they're made from thin materials — gypsum wallboard, plaster and lath, or wood paneling — laid over a framework of studs and joists (see drawing below).

Wall studs, usually 2 by 4 lumber, are structural members that run between a sole plate at the floor and a top plate at the ceiling. Ceiling joists frame the ceiling or upper-story floor.

Screwing your bookshelves or cabinets to studs or joists is the simplest, most secure method of attaching them. If anchoring into the house framing isn't practical or if the wall is masonry, you'll have to use special fasteners.

How to find studs and joists. Studs and joists are spaced at regular intervals — usually 16 or 24 inches on center. Once you've found one stud, locating the rest should be easy.

There are several methods for finding the first stud. One way is to knock firmly on the wall with the heel of your clenched fist. A solid sound means a stud is behind; a hollow sound tells you to keep knocking.

Another method is to look carefully at your paneling or wallboard — it often shows where nails have been driven into studs. If nails don't show, use a stud finder, an inexpensive device with a magnetized needle that dances as it nears a nail head.

If you're still uncertain, drill exploratory holes in a likely but inconspicuous spot with a small bit.

The same methods apply to finding joists. If the ceiling is suspended, push up a section and look for solid wood. If you're working on the top (or only) story of a house, you may be able to crawl into the attic and see the placement of the joists; if necessary, you can even add support blocking between joists.

Special fasteners. For hanging lightweight shelving from wall coverings alone, choose either spreading anchors or toggle bolts (see drawing below). *Spreading anchors*, consisting of a bolt and metal sleeve, are tapped into a predrilled hole. Tightening the bolt expands the sleeve against the wall's back side. You then back out the bolt, slip it through the object to be attached, and retighten the bolt in the sleeve.

Toggle bolts have spring-loaded, winglike toggles that expand once they're through the wall. Drill a hole large enough for the compressed toggles. Pass the bolt through the object to be mounted and attach the toggles; then slide the toggles through the hole — they'll open on the other side and pull up against the back of the wall when you tighten the bolt.

Masonry walls can hold plenty of weight if you use lead shields or expanding anchors. *Lead shields* employ hollow-core, threaded sleeves in tandem with woodscrews or stouter lag screws. Using a masonry bit, drill a hole the diameter of the sleeve and slightly longer, and tap the sleeve in. After slipping the screw through the object to be attached, drive the screw into the sleeve.

More reliable than lead shields, *expanding anchors* feature expanding rings or prongs that grip masonry firmly when the nut is driven home.

INSTALLING CABINETS

You can install cabinets with basic tools, though the work must be done carefully to achieve a professional look. Here's how.

Wall units. To begin the job, locate the wall studs in the area of your new cabinets. Snap a chalkline to mark the studs' centers. Next, lay out the units' top line from the floor (84 inches is standard for wall cabinets). Because floors are seldom completely level, measure in several spots and use the highest mark for your reference point. Trace a line from this mark across the wall, using a carpenter's level as a straightedge.

Then measure down the exact height of the cabinets from the top line and mark this line on the wall. Tack a ledger strip to the wall studs.

With a helper or two, lift the first cabinet into place atop the ledger. Drill pilot holes through the cabinet's nail rail into wall studs; loosely fasten

Hidden Studs & Joists

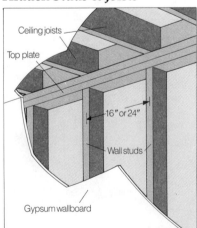

Most wall and ceiling coverings *are supported by studs or joists; whenever possible, fasten your project directly to them.*

Special Fasteners

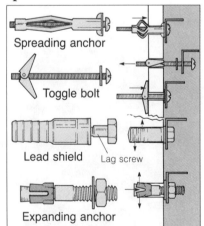

If you can't fasten *your shelves or cabinets to house framing or if your walls are masonry, use one of these fasteners.*

the cabinet to the studs with 3-inch woodscrews or drywall screws and finishing washers.

Check the cabinet carefully for level and plumb. Because walls are seldom exactly plumb, you may have to make some adjustments to enable the cabinet to hang correctly. Bumps or high spots can sometimes be sanded; low spots will need to be shimmed. When all is in order, tighten the screws and recheck with the level.

If your unit includes scribing strips (see page 55) along the sides, you can shave them down to achieve a tight fit. To scribe a cabinet, first position it; then run masking tape down the side to be scribed. Setting the points of a compass with pencil to the widest gap between the scribing strip and wall, run the compass down the wall, as shown below. The wall's irregularities will be transferred to the tape.

Remove the cabinet from the wall and trim the scribing strip to the line with a belt sander or plane. Then reinstall the cabinet.

Adjacent wall units may be joined together on the wall or on the floor; clamp them together with C-clamps, carefully aligning the front edges, and screw together adjacent cabinet sides or faceframes.

Base cabinets. First, remove any baseboard, moldings, or vinyl wall

Marking Reference Lines for Cabinets

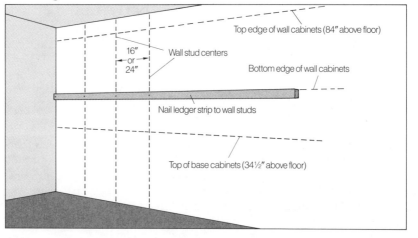

- Top edge of wall cabinets (84″ above floor)
- 16″ or 24″
- Wall stud centers
- Bottom edge of wall cabinets
- Nail ledger strip to wall studs
- Top of base cabinets (34½″ above floor)

base that might interfere with the placement of the cabinets; then locate any wall studs in the area (if you haven't already done so) and mark them as described for wall units.

If your units have a separate kickbase, set it in place. Once it's shimmed level all around, screw it to studs; then add mitered lumber or plywood facing strips (see drawing below) if necessary.

Otherwise, measure up the exact cabinet height off the floor in several spots; then use the highest mark for your reference point. Draw a level line through the mark and across the wall.

If you need to cut an access hole in a cabinet's back or bottom for plumbing

lines or electrical boxes, do so now. Then, with helpers, move the cabinet into position. Check level and plumb carefully — from side to side and front to back — and shim the unit as necessary between the cabinet base and floor. If your cabinet includes scribing strips, trim them as described for wall units.

When the cabinet is aligned, drill pilot holes through the nail rail or case back into the wall studs. Fasten the unit to the studs with 3-inch woodscrews or drywall screws and finishing washers.

Once in place, base cabinets are fastened together like wall cabinets; screw together the adjacent sides or faceframes.

Installing Cabinets: Three Tips

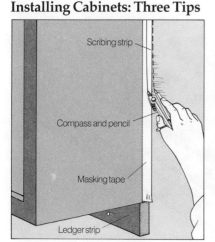

- Scribing strip
- Compass and pencil
- Masking tape
- Ledger strip

To scribe a cabinet to an irregular wall, set a compass for the widest gap and run it along the scribing strip.

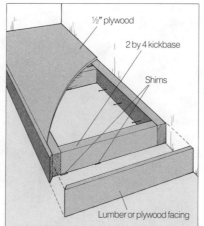

- ½″ plywood
- 2 by 4 kickbase
- Shims
- Lumber or plywood facing

A separate kickbase is easy to install: just shim it level and screw it to wall studs. Facing strips complete the picture.

- Align cabinet fronts exactly
- Pilot hole
- C-clamp

To join two units, clamp them together; then drill pilot holes and screw through adjacent sides or faceframes.

Base cabinets need countertops and your choices are many, including wood, tile, stone, stainless steel, and synthetic marble. But colorful, easy-to-clean plastic laminate remains the most popular material.

Plastic laminate countertops come in two types: post-formed and self-rimmed. Post-formed tops are pre-molded, from curved backsplash to bullnosed front, and can be cut to exact length. The term self-rimmed, on the other hand, really means custom-made. Though a self-rimmed countertop entails some extra work, it allows you to choose from a much greater selection of laminates and to tailor your countertop to your needs. Both post-formed and self-rimmed countertops can be installed with standard woodworking tools and techniques.

Post-formed laminate countertops

Since post-formed countertops come only in standard sizes (usually from 6 to 12 feet), you'll normally need to buy one slightly larger than you need and cut it to length.

Exactly what size do you need? The standard overhang on a laminate top varies between ¾ inch and 1 inch in front and on open ends. Add these dimensions to the dimensions of your cabinet. If you plan to include an endsplash at one or both ends, you generally *subtract* ¾ inch from the length of the countertop on that side.

To cut a countertop with a circular saw, mark the cut line on the back. Mark the top if you're using a handsaw. Use masking tape to protect the cutting line against chipping.

Endsplashes are screwed either directly into the edge of the countertop or into "built-down" wood battens attached to the edge, as shown below. Apply silicone sealant to the surfaces to be joined. Holding the endsplash in place with C-clamps, drill pilot holes, if needed, and drive in the screws.

Endcaps (preshaped strips of matching laminate) are glued to an unfinished end with contact cement or, in some cases, pressed into place with a hot iron. Again, you may first need to build down the edge with wood battens. File the edges of the new strip flush with the top and front edges of the countertop, or use an electric router and laminate-trimming bit.

Countertops, like cabinets, rarely fit uniformly against the back or side walls because the walls are rarely straight. Usually, the back edge of a post-formed countertop comes with a scribing strip that can be trimmed to follow the exact contours of the wall. Follow the instructions on page 71 for scribing cabinets.

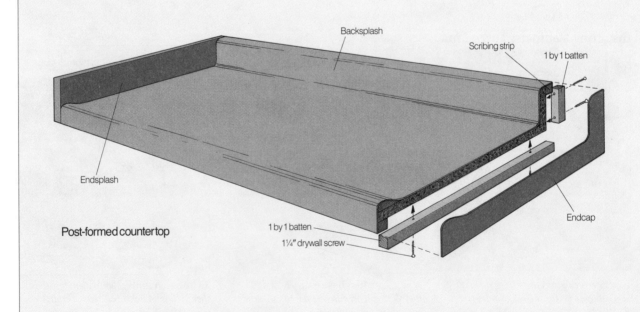

Backsplash

Scribing strip

1 by 1 batten

Endcap

Endsplash

Post-formed countertop

1 by 1 batten

1¼" drywall screw

After positioning the countertop on the frame, fasten it by running screws from below through the cabinet top braces or corner blocks. Use woodscrews just long enough to penetrate ½ inch into the countertop core. Run a bead of silicone sealant along all exposed seams between the countertop and walls; clean up any excess.

If you need to cut a hole in the new countertop for a sink or cooktop, you'll need a saber saw or keyhole saw. See page 24 for details.

Self-rimmed laminate countertops

To build your own top, you'll first need to choose the laminate (¹⁄₁₆ inch is standard for countertops) and cut the core material from ¾-inch plywood or high-density particleboard.

Build down the edges of the core with 1 by 3 battens (see drawing below). To laminate the countertop, follow the instructions below, applying the side and front edge strips first, then the top surface.

Measure each surface to be laminated, adding ¼ inch to the length and width as a margin for error. Score the cutting line first with a sharp utility knife; then cut with a fine-toothed saw blade or laminate cutter.

Apply contact cement to both surfaces to be joined and wait for 20 to 30 minutes — or until the glue is dry but still tacky to touch. Carefully check alignment before joining surfaces: once joined, the laminate cannot be moved. Trim the laminate flush with an electric router equipped with a laminate-trimming bit; or trim it with a block plane and then dress it with a fine-toothed file.

Cover the top surface with a piece of heavy brown wrapping paper and lay the glued side of the laminate down on the paper. The glue, if dry enough, should not stick to the paper. Align all edges; then slowly pull the paper out, pressing the laminate down as you go. (A roller is helpful once the laminate is attached.) On large surfaces, try using two overlapping sheets of paper and work one side at a time.

Backsplashes and endsplashes should be cut from the same core material and then butt-joined to the countertop with sealant and woodscrews. Add a trim piece of soft pine along the edge of the backsplash or endsplash to serve as a scribing strip.

Clean up any rough edges with the file. Remove any excess contact cement with lacquer thinner; then clean the top, following the manufacturer's directions. Finally, install the countertop as described for post-formed tops.

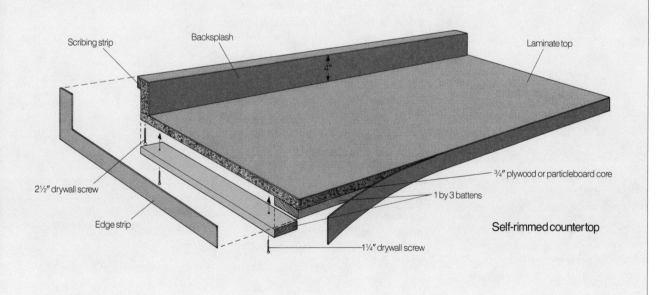

Scribing strip

Backsplash

Laminate top

4"

2½" drywall screw

Edge strip

¾" plywood or particleboard core

1 by 3 battens

1¼" drywall screw

Self-rimmed countertop

PROJECT
IDEAS

In this final chapter, we present a sampler of 31 project ideas—shelves and cabinets that are novel departures from the usual designs. Many of these are specific projects; some are more general ideas. Most are suitable for beginners.

Browse through the drawings and text. If an idea interests you, simply adapt it to your needs and available space. Or perhaps you'll want to borrow a method here and a material there—just be sure your project is based on sound design and technique.

If you have questions about lumber, fasteners, finishes, or basic techniques, you'll find the answers you need in the first two chapters. For specific information on constructing bookshelves and cabinets, such as the proper shelf span for 2 by 10 fir or the best way to join drawer parts, turn back to the appropriate section in the "Design & Assembly" chapter. Before you know it, you'll be turning out projects for every room of your house.

Open Shelf
with
Wood Brackets

Custom-cut wood brackets give a 2 by 10 shelf a solid, classic look. Cut the shelf to length and use scrap pieces for the brackets. Sketch your bracket design on paper, transfer it to wood, and make the first cut; then use this bracket to mark the rest. Notch each one for the 1 by 2 ledger; then shape the bracket fronts as you wish.

To assemble, first nail the ledger to wall studs; then screw the shelf to the brackets so they'll align with every other stud. Nail the unit to the ledger and studs as shown.

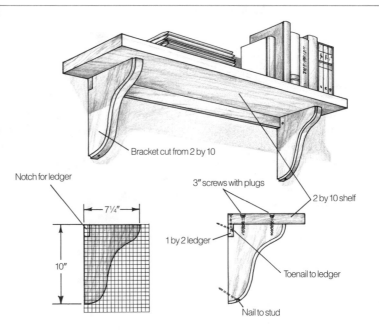

Bracket cut from 2 by 10

Notch for ledger

7¼"

10"

3" screws with plugs

2 by 10 shelf

1 by 2 ledger

Toenail to ledger

Nail to stud

Easy-to-make
Book & Record
Racks

One-inch dowels form the tracks for these adjustable racks.

To make the book rack, cut two 8-inch 1 by 3s and two pieces of hardwood dowel (the length's up to you). You'll also need two 8-inch squares of clear acrylic.

Clamp all acrylic and 1 by 3 pieces together and drill 1-inch holes through all four pieces; then drill ¹⁄₁₆-inch pilot holes through the acrylic and halfway through the wood. On acrylic only, enlarge the ¹⁄₁₆-inch holes with a ⁷⁄₆₄-inch bit. Screw the acrylic to the wood; then insert the dowels.

To build the record rack, cut 1 by 12 hardwood into three 12½-inch-long pieces. Next, cut four pieces of dowel.

Clamp the large pieces together and drill four 1-inch holes. Slide the pieces onto the dowels and glue the dowels to the end pieces. Drill ⅜-inch holes from the edges of the end pieces into the dowels. Glue ⅜-inch dowels in the holes, saw off the excess, and sand flush.

Design: William Crosby.

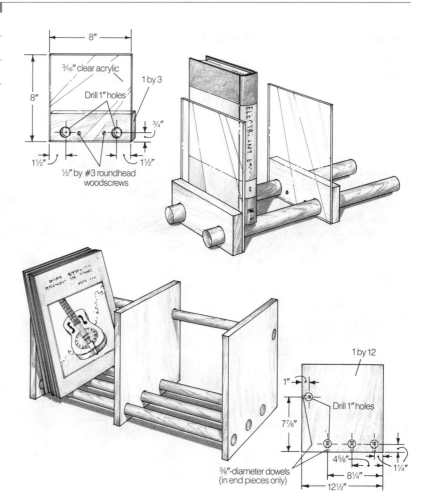

8"

8"

³⁄₁₆" clear acrylic

Drill 1" holes

1 by 3

¾"

1½"

1½"

½" by #3 roundhead woodscrews

1 by 12

1"

Drill 1" holes

7⅞"

4⅝"

8¼"

1¼"

12½"

⅜"-diameter dowels (in end pieces only)

STURDY SHELF WITH HIDDEN MOUNTING

The clean lines of this bookshelf system come from its simple construction and out-of-view mounting scheme.

Cut each shelf from a 2 by 10, sizing the pieces to align with wall studs at both ends. Miter the corners; for extra strength, add dowels as shown.

Near the top of each end piece, rout a ¼-inch-deep recess to receive a keyhole plate. At the appropriate height, attach screws to the studs as shown.

Paint all shelves white. Fit the screw heads into the keyhole slots and lower each shelf into place.

Design: T. Scott MacGillivray.

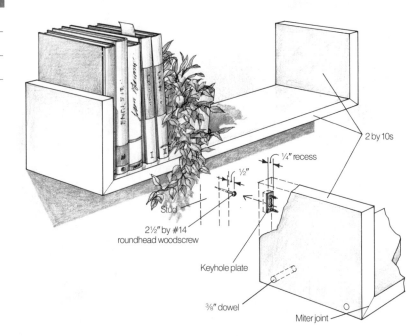

2 by 10s

¼" recess

½"

Stud

2½" by #14 roundhead woodscrew

Keyhole plate

⅜" dowel

Miter joint

FLOATING SHELVES: TWO VERSIONS

Both of these shelf systems "float" on invisible supports—one on dowels, the other on steel rods.

To make the first version, rip 1 ⅝-inch dowels to within an inch of one end, square off the cut, and then trim the flat portion to the exact width of the shelf. Every 12 inches along a 2 by 6 ledger, drill a 1 ⅝-inch hole 1 inch deep as shown. Glue the dowels into their holes and screw into them from the back. Then fasten the 2 by 6 to wall studs.

Shelves are 1 by 10s with 1 by 2 trim. Glue and nail the shelves to the dowels (brace the dowels from below).

The second version features ¾-inch steel rods set into holes drilled 3 inches into wall studs. The 17-inch-deep shelves are particleboard above and below with lumber strips in the middle; leave a gap where each rod will go. Laminate the shelves; then screw maple trim to the front and side edges. Simply slip each shelf into place.

Design: James and Roberta Cutler.

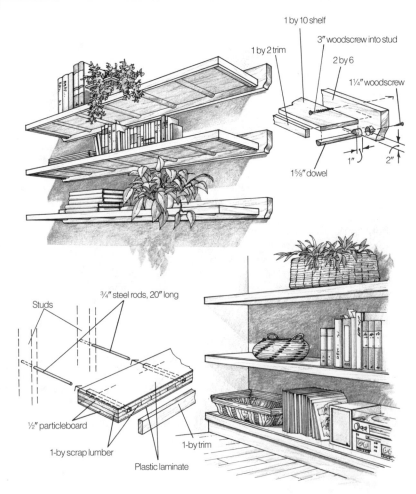

1 by 10 shelf

3" woodscrew into stud

1 by 2 trim

2 by 6

1¼" woodscrew

¼" recess

1⅝" dowel

1"

2"

Studs

¾" steel rods, 20" long

½" particleboard

1-by scrap lumber

Plastic laminate

1-by trim

Glass Display Shelves

Nothing shows off lightweight display objects like glass, and these glass and maple shelves are no exception.

Maple 2 by 2s form the uprights. Shelf supports are cut from 2 by 2s as well; taper them as shown. Glue them inside dadoes in the uprights and add screws as shown. Apply penetrating oil or varnish.

Screw the maple assemblies to wall studs. Add the ¼-inch plate glass shelves. A dab of silicone sealant helps keep the shelves stationary.

Design: Frank Israel and Douglas Quick.

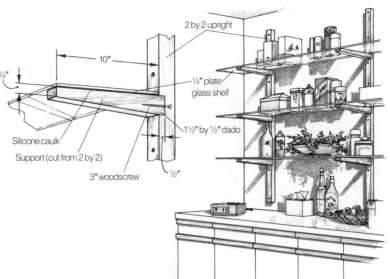

A Bookshelf as Wide as the Room

Sliding bookends give this room-wide bookshelf flexibility for both light-weight storage and display.

Cut a vertical-grain Douglas fir 1 by 12 to the width of the room; then rip a 2¼-inch-wide piece off one edge to serve as the front lip. Next, shape a ¾-by ⅜-inch rabbet in the lip's back edge. In the remaining piece, center and cut two 2-inch-wide slots, leaving a solid 6-inch bridge section in the middle and 6 inches at each end. Scribe and cut a 2-inch semicircle at both ends of each slot. Glue and nail the lip to the shelf.

Next, cut a 1 by 2 ledger to the room's width and two smaller pieces for the end walls. Anchor the ledgers to studs (you may need toggle bolts for the ends). Nail the shelf to the ledgers.

To make four bookends, cut a 1 by 4 into four 9-inch pieces. Mark one book-end for 1-inch-deep notches. Clamp the bookends together and cut all the notches at once. Round off the corners.

Design: Peter Whiteley.

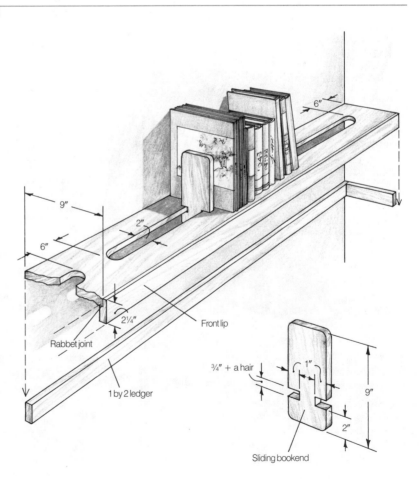

TRACKS & BRACKETS—
HOW TO MOUNT THEM,
HOW TO HIDE THEM

Metal tracks and brackets have become one of the most common ways to mount open shelves. Why the popularity? They're adjustable, easy to install, widely available, and inexpensive.

Brackets are available in many different styles and finishes. The most common brackets are sized for 8-, 10-, or 12-inch-wide lumber. Track lengths vary from 12 inches to ceiling height.

On these two pages, we show you how to mount tracks and brackets and then offer several suggestions for customizing your installation.

Mounting tracks & brackets

To install tracks and brackets, first decide where the shelves should go. The tracks should be spaced from 16 to 32 inches apart, depending on your shelf design and load (see page 45), and should be fastened into wall studs with screws. If the wall is made from gypsum wallboard, plaster, or paneling, locate the studs behind; if the wall is masonry, you'll need special fasteners (in either case, see page 70 for details). If you need to cut tracks to length, use a hacksaw; just be sure the slots line up exactly from piece to piece.

Place the first track in position, drill a small pilot hole through one screw hole, and drive in a screw, as shown at left. Leave the screw slightly loose so you can move the track. Next, check for plumb with a carpenter's level and mark along the track's edge for reference. Align the track with your marks and drill the remaining pilot holes. Then install and tighten all screws.

Insert a bracket in the first track; then place a bracket in the matching slot of another track. Lift the second track into position, place a shelf across the brackets—you may need a helper for this—and put a level on the shelf as shown. Level the shelf by moving the track; then mark the track's top and bottom on the wall. Install the second track as you did the first. Add any other tracks in the same manner.

Finally, install the brackets, locking them into place with a slight downward pull; if they don't seat, tap them lightly with a hammer.

Dressing up shelf hardware

Perhaps you'd like a warmer, more custom look than bare shelf hardware provides. Here are several ways to combine the efficiency of standard hardware with the character of custom units.

To partially hide standard brackets, recess their tips. Pick the next smallest bracket than the "right" size for your shelf width and drill ¼-inch-diameter holes where bracket tips will meet shelf bottoms. To take the

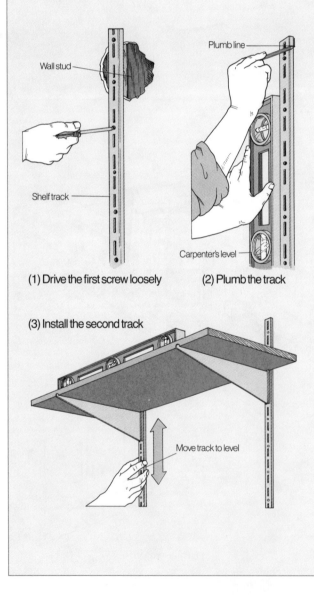

Wall stud

Shelf track

(1) Drive the first screw loosely

Plumb line

Carpenter's level

(2) Plumb the track

(3) Install the second track

Move track to level

process one step further, you can add overhanging lips to shelf fronts.

If you're installing glass shelves, cut off the tips entirely and glue a small rubber or felt pad to the glass as shown.

Grooved uprights mounted to the wall dress up tracks and brackets. Cut 1 by 2s, 2 by 2s, or similar lumber to track length; then cut grooves to inset the tracks flush with the surface of each upright (you'll need a router or table saw).

You can also install the uprights and tracks away from the wall, facing the brackets inward. This hides the tracks completely—you see only solid wood. Pressure devices or L-brackets (see page 47) hold the uprights in position between the ceiling and floor.

No power tools? Rather than inset tracks, hide them between adjoining wood strips. Choose molding, trim, or lath that's about the same thickness as the tracks.

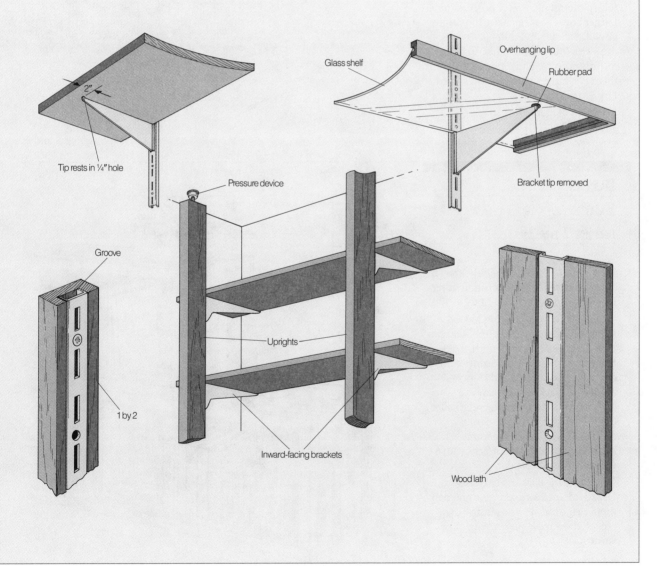

2"

Tip rests in ¼" hole

Glass shelf

Overhanging lip

Rubber pad

Bracket tip removed

Pressure device

Groove

1 by 2

Uprights

Inward-facing brackets

Wood lath

INTERLOCKING
PINE
CRATES

These trim pine boxes interlock to form any number of solid, adaptable units. Build them from kiln-dried 1 by 3s and 1 by 12s, glue, and 4-penny finishing nails.

Cut all pieces and sand before assembly. Glue and nail the first 1 by 3 flush with the sides and back edge of the 1 by 12s. Using another 1 by 3 as a spacer, attach the second 1 by 3 and remove the spacer. Repeat on the other side, staggering the 1 by 3s as shown.

Set the nail heads and fill; finish with penetrating resin or polyurethane. Larger boxes—*exactly* twice the height or width shown in the detail drawing—will interact smoothly. To house records, look for wider pine boards; cut them 12½ inches long and add a third 1 by 3 to the top.

Design: Roger Flanagan.

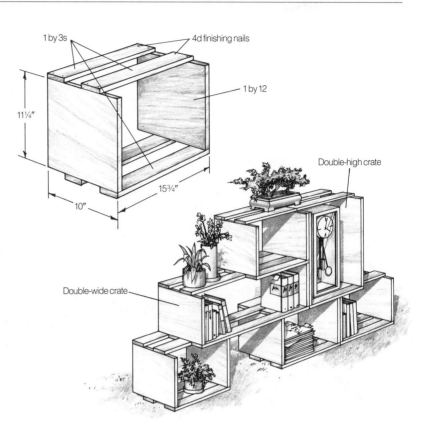

1 by 3s 4d finishing nails

11¼"

1 by 12

10" 15¾"

Double-high crate

Double-wide crate

BOXES
BUILT
FROM 2 BY 2S

Fancy box joints these are not—they're simply stacked-up rows of alternating Douglas fir and redwood 2 by 2s.

Start with clear, kiln-dried wood, selecting the straightest pieces you can find. Cut the 2 by 2s to length: make the redwood rows 36 and 16 inches long; cut the fir pieces to 33 and 13 inches. Then start stacking, one row at a time. Glue adjoining edges and ends; nail down each corner with 8-penny finishing nails. When the frame is complete, smooth the surfaces with a plane and/or belt sander.

To make the back, rip two redwood 1 by 10s to 8 inches wide; glue and nail them to the box. Finish-sand all the pieces; then apply penetrating oil or varnish.

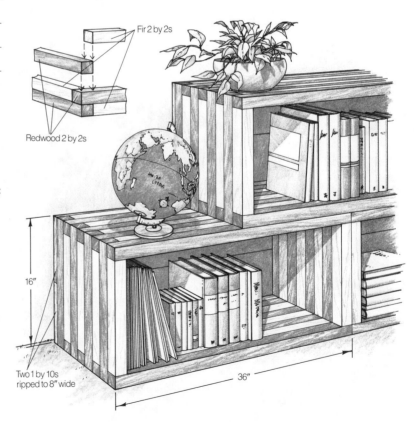

Fir 2 by 2s

Redwood 2 by 2s

16"

Two 1 by 10s ripped to 8" wide

36"

STACKING BOOKCASE MODULES

Though it looks like a formal bookcase, this set of stacking modules breaks down into individual "shelves." As your book collection grows, just add another unit or two.

To build a module, first cut the 1 by 12 sides and shelf and the 1 by 4 back slats to length. (We show two side heights; the taller size is for oversize books and phonograph records.) Then shape dadoes in the sides for the shelf; glue and nail the joints. Glue on the back slats and nail them through the sides.

Next, drill holes for the $5/16$- by 1-inch dowels (oversize $11/32$-inch holes make it simpler to add or remove dowels). For a finished look at the top of your stack, add a 1 by 12 cap as shown. Sand all pieces; then apply the finish of your choice.

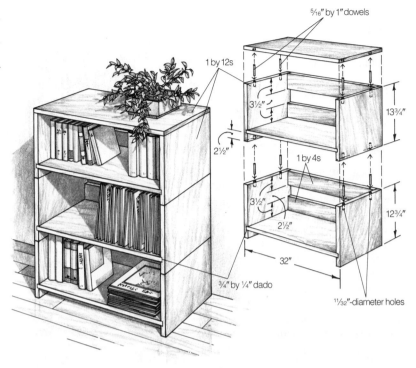

A RACK FOR A MAGAZINE COLLECTION

They normally scatter all over the house: magazines, catalogs, and paperbacks. This handy rack keeps them corralled—and takes advantage of doorside space in a family room, breakfast nook, study, or bathroom.

Uprights and shelves are 1 by 3s assembled "ladder-style." After cutting them to size, round off the tops of the uprights and dado them. (For most magazines, 12-inch-high shelves and 7-inch-high acrylic strips are sufficient, but you can vary the dimensions as desired.) Glue and nail the shelves to the uprights. Add nail rails.

Sand and finish; then screw $1/4$-inch acrylic pieces in place. Fasten the unit to wall studs or anchor it with toggle bolts.

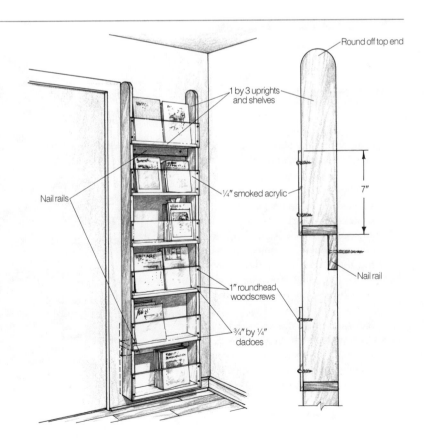

SCALE IT UP OR DOWN

Four square holes near the corners of each shelf make this bookcase easy to build, adjust, and knock down. Make it as tall as you like.

Cut each 11- by 29½-inch shelf from ½-inch plywood. Then cut a 1⅝-inch square from each corner; band all four edges with mitered 1 by 2s, extending them past the cutouts to create the square holes. Drill holes for dowel pegs in the 2 by 2 uprights as shown.

To assemble, screw 8-inch spacers to the bottom of each pair of uprights, as shown. Add the dowels and shelves, a row at a time. Finish with spacers at the top. To brace the unit, screw the top and bottom shelves to the uprights. Then screw through the back lip of the top shelf into wall studs.

Design: Henry Wood.

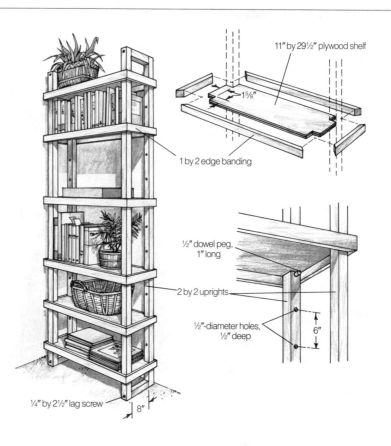

11" by 29½" plywood shelf

1⅝"

1 by 2 edge banding

½" dowel peg, 1" long

2 by 2 uprights

½"-diameter holes, ½" deep

6"

¼" by 2½" lag screw

8"

KNOCK-DOWN WITH A BUILT-IN LOOK

This sophisticated-looking wall unit is really a simple system of interconnected boxes and adjustable shelves.

Build the box frames and shelves from 1 by 12 clear pine or fir; secure joints with glue and finishing nails. Box backs are ¼-inch shop-grade birch plywood. Drill ¼- by ⅜-inch holes for shelf pegs or pins, as shown. The holes inside the boxes are spaced 1½ inches from the edge; on the outside, space them 2 inches from the edge so they're offset from the inside holes.

Sand and finish the boxes and shelves with penetrating oil. Using two woodscrews for each, anchor the tall boxes to wall studs through the top of the backs. Add the shelves and smaller boxes.

Design: Don Vandervort.

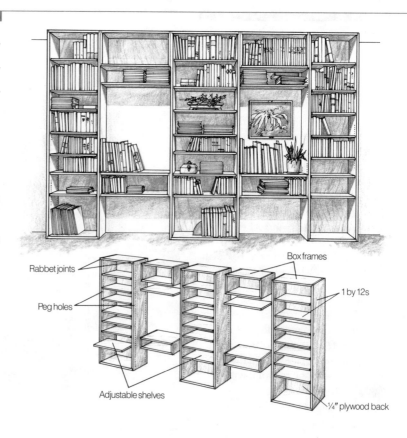

Box frames

Rabbet joints

Peg holes

1 by 12s

Adjustable shelves

¼" plywood back

SHELVES IN PREGROOVED PLYWOOD

Dozens of grooves in this unit's plywood sides provide support for adjustable shelves—and you don't have to cut a single dado. Just buy ⅝-inch redwood exterior siding panels with the grooves already milled on 4-inch centers. (Avoid panels with a heavy preservative odor.)

Begin the project by cutting the 2 by 3 fir frame pieces to 80⅜ and 11 inches. Then cut the ⅝-inch siding, matching the overlapping and underlapping edges as shown. Cut off the shorter overlapping flange of the 15½- by 48-inch panels. Also cut the ⅜-inch plywood shelves to size.

Assemble the three 2 by 3 frames, using glue and corrugated fasteners where the plywood will hide them. Interlock one 32-inch and one 48-inch panel on one of the frames, leaving the proper ⅜-inch groove where they meet. The short top panel's squarely cut edge should be flush with the top; align the pair's back edges with the frame's back edge. Let the plywood fall short at the frame's bottom. Use a shelf to line up the grooves of each remaining frame's panels.

Glue and nail ½- by ¾-inch molding to the front and side edges of the top panel. Align the frames by sliding shelves into the grooves; then tack the top in position and drill ⅛-inch holes through the top into the frames. Remove the top and drive ¼-inch by 1½-inch hanger bolts into the holes until about an inch protrudes. Enlarge the top panel's holes to ¼ inch, slip it over the bolts, and add washers and nuts.

Position the back with its overlapping flange at the top and fit the bottom shelves into the back's grooves to ensure proper alignment; fasten the back in place with 1¼-inch drywall screws. Anchor the bottom shelves to the uprights with L-brackets.

Glue and nail molding to the front edges of the shelves, overlapping the molding as shown.

Design: Donald Wm. MacDonald.

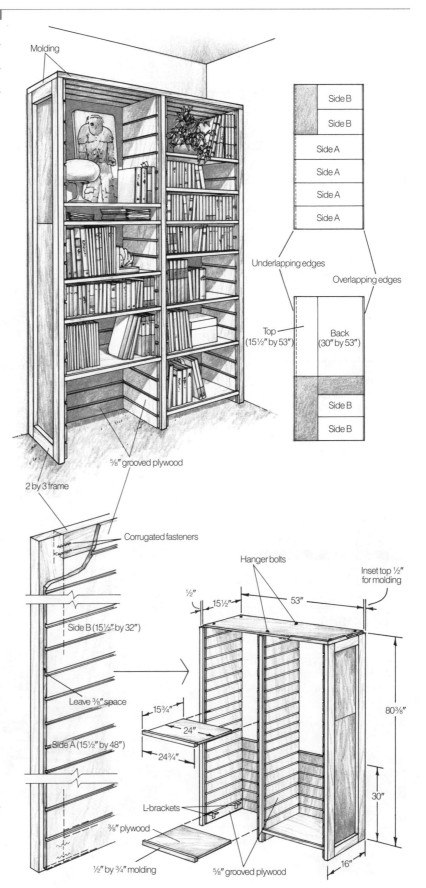

Molding

Side B
Side B
Side A
Side A
Side A
Side A

Underlapping edges

Overlapping edges

Top (15½" by 53")

Back (30" by 53")

Side B
Side B

⅝" grooved plywood

2 by 3 frame

Corrugated fasteners

Hanger bolts

Inset top ½" for molding

½"
15½"
53"

Side B (15½" by 32")

Leave ⅜" space

15¾"
24"

24¾"

Side A (15½" by 48")

80⅜"

30"

L-brackets

⅜" plywood

½" by ¾" molding

⅝" grooved plywood

16"

EASY-TO-BUILD REDWOOD SHELVES

Rough redwood gives this project its woodsy character. Uprights of 2 by 10 lumber support 1 by 10 shelves on 1-inch hardwood dowels.

To begin, cut the uprights, shelves, and dowels to length: the uprights should be ¼ inch shorter than ceiling height; the shelves are 32 inches long, and dowels measure 3½ inches long.

Next, drill 1-inch holes for the dowels in the uprights. (You can adjust the measurements shown to suit your needs.) Center the dowels in the holes.

If desired, sand the redwood—just enough to prevent splinters. A satin polyurethane finish will preserve the rough texture.

The uprights can be anchored to the wall or ceiling; attach L-brackets with 2½-inch woodscrews if you've found a stud or joist, or with spreading anchors if you haven't. Add L-brackets to the undersides of lower shelves, as shown, for extra stability.

Design: Roger Flanagan.

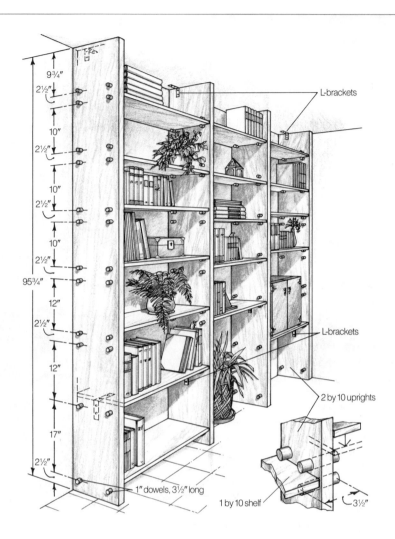

SHELVES ON LADDERS

Ladderlike supports, built from fir 2 by 4s and 1⅜-inch wooden closet rod, carry the weight of 2 by 10 shelves.

Cut the 2 by 4s into four equal lengths and shape ½-inch-deep recesses in them for the 10½-inch-long rungs, as shown. Secure the rungs with 3-inch woodscrews. Add a 9½-inch piece of 2 by 4 at the top of each ladder and attach the ladders to joists as shown.

Cut each shelf 60 inches long; the weight of the shelves will keep them in place. Add an intermediate ladder for shelves longer than 5 feet.

Design: Fred Repass.

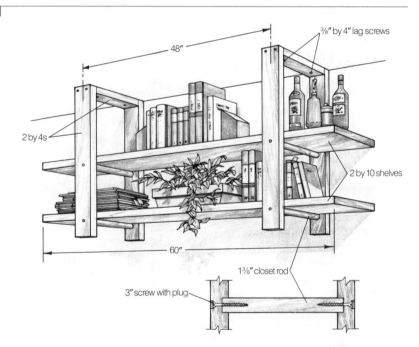

A CAT'S CRADLE OF 2 BY 2s

If you can drill, you can build this wall system. All you need is a good supply of clear redwood 2 by 2s, four 15-inch lengths of ¼-inch threaded rod, and ⁵⁄₁₆- by 15-inch dowels for all remaining intersections.

After cutting the pieces to length, lay out one layer of each horizontal and vertical 2 by 2; drill ¹¹⁄₃₂-inch holes where pieces intersect. Use these pieces as templates to drill through all the other 2 by 2s except the front and back outside verticals; drill only ¾ inch into these. Where rods are used instead of dowels, drill ⅝-inch-diameter holes into the outside verticals so they will fit over rod-end nuts. Finish the redwood with penetrating oil.

To assemble the unit, push 2 by 2s over dowels and rods; tighten the nuts at rod ends. Then put a little glue on all dowel ends and slip the outside verticals into place. Anchor the unit to the wall or ceiling with L-brackets.

Design: Richard W. Robinson.

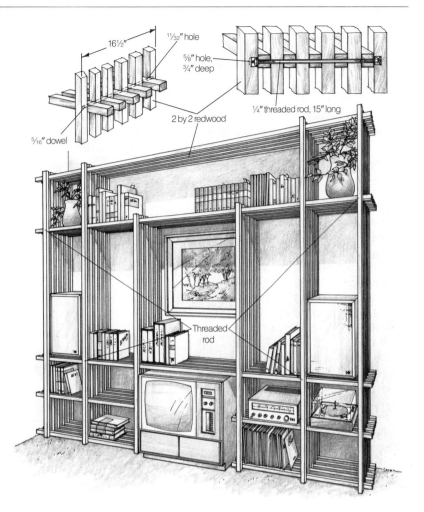

16½" — ¹¹⁄₃₂" hole — ⅝" hole, ¾" deep — ¼" threaded rod, 15" long — 2 by 2 redwood — ⁵⁄₁₆" dowel — Threaded rod

HEAVY-DUTY GARAGE PLATFORM

Luggage and other bulky items line up along these secure shelves, which take advantage of high wall space in garages or basements.

The 30-inch-deep shelves are simply two layers of plywood glued together and trimmed with 1 by 2s on front and side edges. They sit atop 1 by 4 ledger strips screwed to wall studs. The fronts are supported by threaded rods secured with couplings and eye bolts tied to screw hooks in ceiling joists or rafters. For a neater look, center wider trim on the plywood edges to hide the nuts and washers.

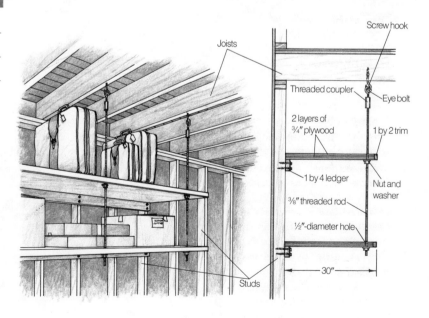

Joists — Screw hook — Threaded coupler — Eye bolt — 2 layers of ¾" plywood — 1 by 2 trim — 1 by 4 ledger — Nut and washer — ⅜" threaded rod — ½"-diameter hole — Studs — 30"

TWO-WAY
ROOM
DIVIDER

A basic bookcase becomes a combination bookshelf and room divider when the frame is widened and the back removed. The addition of plywood facings creates the look of a solid wall while leaving separate niches and pass-throughs for books and display objects.

The unit shown is 5 feet tall by 6 feet long and 12¾ inches wide, but dimensions can easily be altered. Assemble the plywood frame with glue and finishing nails. Cut the shelves, which rest on tracks and clips, from 1 by 12 lumber. Face them along exposed edges with 1 by 2 trim.

Cut plywood facings to add where desired; the facings should fit flush with the edges of the frame. Glue the facings and nail into them through the uprights.

Then trim both sides of the divider with 1 by 2 faceframes. Fill nail holes, sand, and finish with varnish or enamel. If the unit is over 5 feet tall, one end should be anchored to a wall.

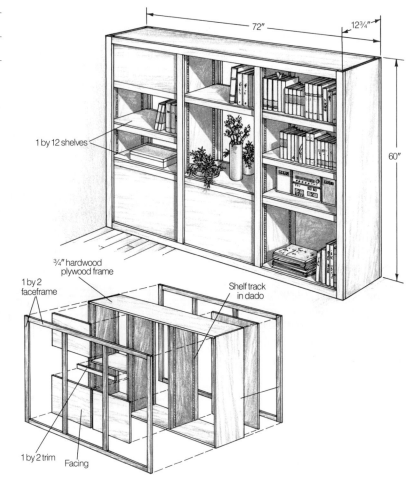

1 by 12 shelves

72"

12¾"

60"

¾" hardwood plywood frame

1 by 2 faceframe

Shelf track in dado

1 by 2 trim

Facing

LIGHTING UP
SHELVES
& CABINETS

Whatever objects your shelves or cabinets hold, carefully placed light fixtures can give them a life of their own.

Recessed downlights spotlight individual objects; to house one, either cut a ceiling hole or build a soffit as shown. *Mini-tracks* are more flexible: mount them with a screwdriver and add fixtures where desired. Place *fluorescent strips* along the lips of shelves or in a light box with a plastic diffusing panel.

Some of these fixtures can be plugged right into a wall outlet; others require a separate housing box.

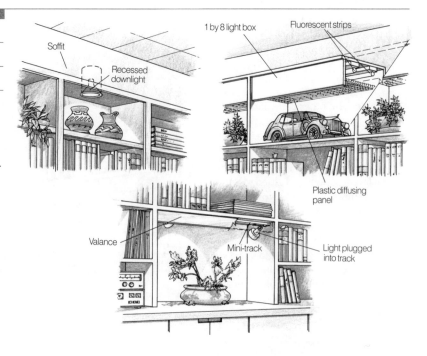

Soffit

Recessed downlight

1 by 8 light box

Fluorescent strips

Plastic diffusing panel

Valance

Mini-track

Light plugged into track

A Cabinet Built for a Corner

This triangular cabinet utilizes a neglected corner, yet cuts off less than 2 feet of floor space.

First, cut the 30- by 71-inch plywood sides; rip one long edge of each at a 45° angle—the inside width should be 29 inches. Cut the triangular shelves as shown. Also cut a 71-inch length of ¾-inch quarter-round molding.

Glue and nail the molding to the long, square-cut edge of one side piece. With a helper, stand this piece upright, butt the other side to the molding, and glue and nail them together.

Next, add the larger triangular shelves, nailing through the sides. Then add the remaining shelves. Countersink the nails, fill the holes, and sand.

Cut and assemble the 1 by 4 faceframe as shown. Centering 1¼-inch-wide decorative trim on the 1 by 4s, glue and nail it in place. Shape ¾- by ⅜-inch rabbets in the top back edge of each piece of 1¼-inch shelf trim. Finally, cut the plywood doors, making them ⅛ inch smaller than the openings in the frame.

Mount narrow strips of scrap wood along the shell's top, as shown, and under the larger middle and bottom shelves. Position the faceframe and screw through the strips to draw the faceframe tightly against the shell. Angle other screws through the outside edge of the shell into the back of the faceframe. Miter the ends of the three shelf trim pieces to fit against the sides of the shell; glue them to the shelf fronts. Finally, add the hinged doors.

Install ¼-inch plate glass doors on the top section, if desired, sizing the glass so each piece has ⅛-inch clearance from the faceframe. Two sets of pivot hinges clamp to the glass and turn in holes drilled in the frame, as shown. Metal strike plates near the upper inside corners lock the doors against a double-barreled magnetic latch. To mount the latch, center and screw a small birch block to the frame.

Design: Peter Whiteley.

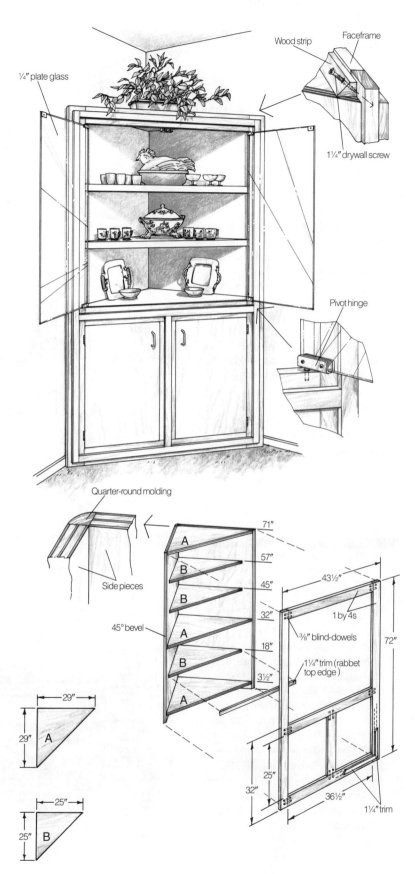

¼″ plate glass

Wood strip

Faceframe

1¼″ drywall screw

Pivot hinge

Quarter-round molding

Side pieces

45° bevel

71″

57″

45″

32″

18″

3½″

A

B

B

A

B

A

43½″

1 by 4s

⅜″ blind-dowels

1¼″ trim (rabbet top edge)

72″

25″

32″

36½″

1¼″ trim

29″

29″

A

25″

25″

B

A Combination Cabinet/Island/ Serving Cart

When stored under the counter, this unit is simply another kitchen base cabinet. But pulled from its hiding place, it becomes an island work station, chopping block, and service cart all in one.

First, assemble the front faceframe, gluing and blind-doweling the joints. Then build the side faceframes as shown. Cut the deck and intermediate shelf from ¾-inch plywood; then attach the faceframes with glue and 6-penny finishing nails. Cut the butcher-block top to size and assemble it flush with the top edges of the faceframes. Add 1 by 3 lips to plywood edges.

Mount heavy-duty casters on spacer blocks as required. Leaving ½-inch clearance at the bottom so the cart rolls smoothly, attach an apron to the cabinet front; align it with adjoining kickbases.

Finally, build and hang the doors, sand all parts, and finish the cart to blend in with its surroundings.

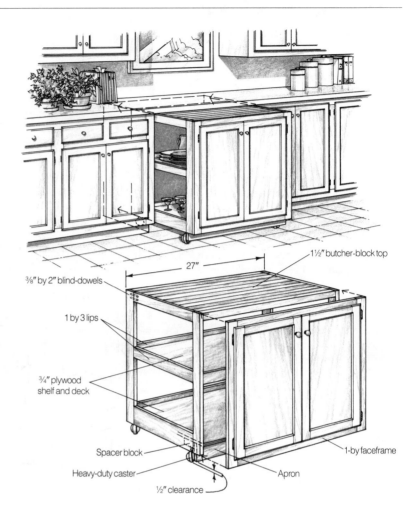

3⁄8" by 2" blind-dowels
1½" butcher-block top
27"
1 by 3 lips
¾" plywood shelf and deck
Spacer block
1-by faceframe
Heavy-duty caster
Apron
½" clearance

A Cabinet Just for Spices

Finding enough space for herbs and spices can be quite a challenge. This trim spice cabinet can help. With its doors closed, the 25-inch-high cabinet is just 20 inches wide; when the two 3-inch-deep doors open on their brass-plated piano hinges, its width doubles.

Build the cabinet frames and doors from ¾-inch cherry as shown. The adjustable shelves and front lips are ¼-inch stock; add an extra set of lips near the bottom of each frame. Finish the cabinet with penetrating oil; anchor it to the wall with toggle bolts.

Design: Don Gerber.

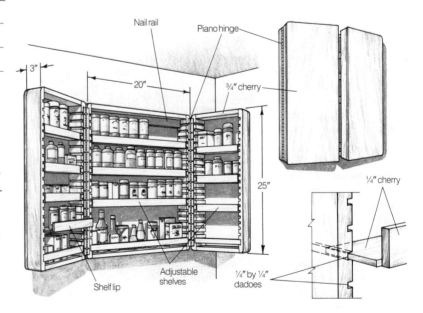

Nail rail
Piano hinge
¾" cherry
3"
20"
25"
¼" cherry
Shelf lip
Adjustable shelves
¼" by ¼" dadoes

WINE
BY THE
DRAWERFUL

This handy rack is like a chest of drawers for wine. Mounted on heavy-duty drawer guides, each level pulls out for easy access to bottles.

To make two front drawer rails, drill 1¼-inch-diameter holes in the center of a 1 by 6; then rip it in half. Rip another 1 by 6 for the rear supports; then shape 1½-inch-deep Vs, as shown. Join front and rear rails to plywood side strips, leaving enough clearance for your drawer guides. The drawers shown are 14 inches deep and hold 10 bottles each.

Next, construct a case for your drawers from ¾-inch plywood or edge-joined solid lumber. Sand all components; then finish the case and drawers as desired. Fasten your frame to wall studs or ceiling joists; then mount the drawers on heavy-duty, full-extension guides so each wine drawer slides all the way out.

Design: John Hamilton and George Kelce.

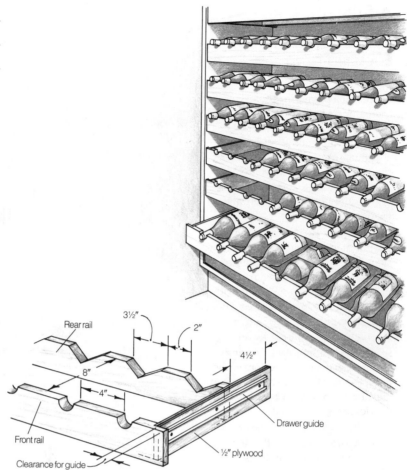

Rear rail

Front rail

Clearance for guide

3½"

2"

8"

4"

4½"

Drawer guide

½" plywood

THE BASIC
BUILT-IN
BREADBOARD

No kitchen is complete without at least one built-in breadboard.

The best breadboards are edge-joined strips of ¾-inch hardwood (maple is a popular choice), faced in front and back with lumber that matches the cabinet faceframe. Plane or belt-sand all joints flush.

To install the breadboard, cut a slot ⅛ inch wider and longer than the board in the faceframe's top rail. Shape a ¹³⁄₁₆-by-⅜-inch dado in two hardwood strips; screw them to the carcase as shown, using filler strips as required to align them with the opening.

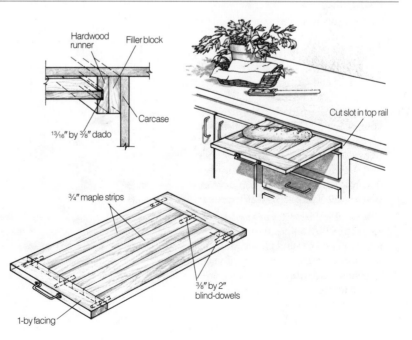

Hardwood runner

Filler block

Carcase

¹³⁄₁₆" by ⅜" dado

Cut slot in top rail

¾" maple strips

⅜" by 2" blind-dowels

1-by facing

Space is at a premium in most bathrooms, and a built-in cabinet recessed between wall studs can provide needed storage without taking over the room.

Although you could fit a very narrow cabinet between studs, in most cases you'll have to remove a part of one middle stud and then reframe the opening.

For starters, locate the studs in the area (for help, see page 70). Check for signs of electrical wiring or plumbing. If all is clear, mark the inside edges of the studs you'll keep; also mark the top and bottom lines at the height you want the cabinet, adding 3½ inches extra at the top and 1½ inches at the bottom for the new header and sill.

Cut away the wall covering along the lines. For gypsum wallboard or paneling, use a keyhole or saber saw. For plaster or tile, cut carefully along the lines with a cold chisel and soft-headed hammer (protect your eyes); then cut the backing and pull it off. Use a hammer to knock off any fire blocks; then, with a handsaw, cut the stud squarely along the top and bottom lines. Pry it carefully away from the wall covering on the other side.

Make the header as shown; then toenail it inside the opening. Cut a 2 by 4 sill to the same length and nail it in place (flat) at the bottom of the opening.

Construct the cabinet frame from 1 by 6 lumber, making it ¼ inch less in height and width than the size of your opening. Then nail on a ¼-inch plywood back. Drill holes for shelf pegs or pins in each side. Add doors, if desired (the mirrored doors shown overlap the fixed shelf slightly, so they don't require pulls). Sand all exposed surfaces and finish.

Position the cabinet in the opening, shimming it level and plumb, and nail it to the framing with 6-penny finishing nails. Add trim around the opening, mitering the corners. Finally, add glass or wood shelves.

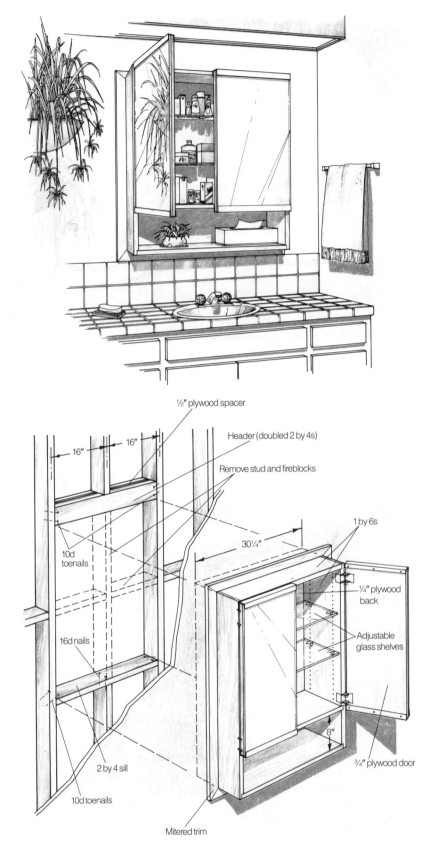

½" plywood spacer

Header (doubled 2 by 4s)

Remove stud and fireblocks

16"   16"

10d toenails

16d nails

30¼"

1 by 6s

¼" plywood back

Adjustable glass shelves

8"

¾" plywood door

2 by 4 sill

10d toenails

Mitered trim

A Custom Filing Cabinet

This filing cabinet features the warm look of birch. The drawers are tailored to standard hanging files (for legal-size files, increase the width).

Build the frame from plywood and hardboard as shown. Then nail on the kickbase and 1 by 3 back brace. Cover the edges with birch veneer tape, mitering the corners.

Assemble the drawers next, leaving clearance for heavy-duty, full-extension side guides (we've allowed ½ inch on each side). For the runners, rabbet ½-inch molding as shown and screw it to the drawer sides. Cut out the decorative fronts.

Finish-sand all pieces and apply penetrating oil to the case and drawer fronts. Mount the drawers and add the fronts and drawer pulls.

Design: Bill Oetinger.

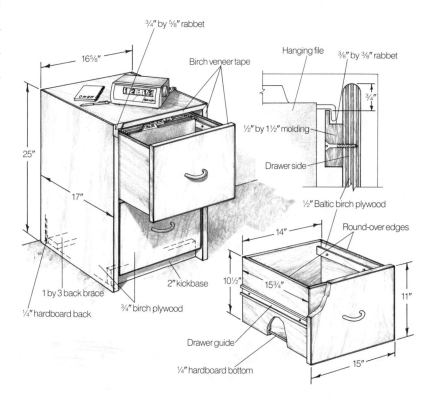

¾" by ⅝" rabbet
Birch veneer tape
Hanging file
⅜" by ⅜" rabbet
16⅝"
25"
17"
½" by 1½" molding
Drawer side
½" Baltic birch plywood
Round-over edges
1 by 3 back brace
¼" hardboard back
2" kickbase
¾" birch plywood
14"
10½"
15¾"
11"
Drawer guide
¼" hardboard bottom
15"

A Stand for a Computer Printer

This cabinet not only houses your printer but also lets you store a full box of fanfold paper on the infeed shelf; your printout can restack on the outfeed shelf.

First, cut all plywood pieces to size; also cut cable slots in the back and a 45° angle on the baffle. Shape the sides as shown. Then bevel all exposed edges and the bottom back edge of the top shelf. Drill a ⅜-inch-deep dowel hole on the inside of each side piece and cut the dowel to length.

Glue and screw the apron to the bottom shelf; attach one side piece and add the remaining shelves. Holding the dowel in place, attach the second side. Add the baffle and back and mount the casters. Fill all holes and voids, sand, and finish as desired.

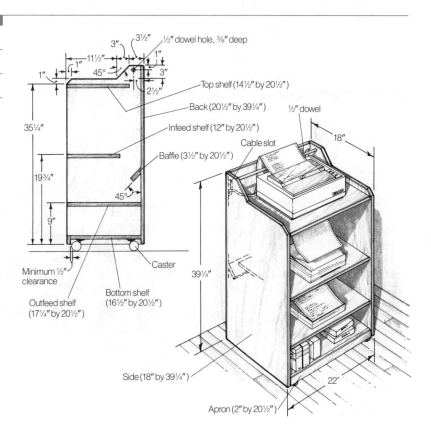

½" dowel hole, ⅜" deep
3"
3½"
11½"
1"
45°
1"
3"
2½"
35¼"
19¾"
9"
45°
Top shelf (14½" by 20½")
Back (20½" by 39¼")
Infeed shelf (12" by 20½")
Baffle (3½" by 20½")
½" dowel
18"
Cable slot
Minimum ½" clearance
Caster
39¼"
22"
Outfeed shelf (17¼" by 20½")
Bottom shelf (16½" by 20½")
Side (18" by 39¼")
Apron (2" by 20½")

IDEAS FOR
DOOR &
DRAWER PULLS

Though you can find all kinds of door and drawer pulls, shaping your own adds a special touch to a project.

The drawer cutouts shown are easy to cut with a saber or coping saw. For a smoother look, round-over the cut edges.

To make the rings, cut squares of ¼-inch wood (oak flooring works well), drill a ¾-inch hole in each, and round off the ends as shown. Glue them into ¼-inch-wide kerfs in door or drawer fronts.

Integral rails create a pleasing horizontal look. Cut a 45° bevel as shown; then cut the stock to length, and glue and nail the rails in place.

If your drawers have false fronts, try the round recesses. Drill holes through the decorative fronts; then rout a finger pull along each back edge, as shown. Face the area of the false front that will be exposed with hardwood veneer squares or stain it; then attach the decorative front.

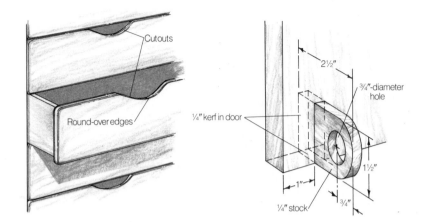

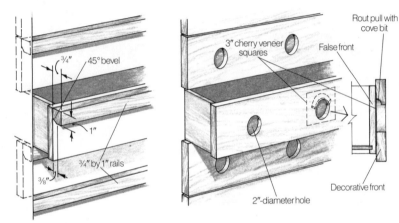

CABINET
ORGANIZERS:
TWO TYPES

Finding the right bowl or frying pan can be frustrating if everything is thrown together in one large cabinet. Pull-out "shelves" concealed behind cabinet doors are an effective remedy: build them as shown and then mount them on heavy-duty, full-extension drawer guides.

Flat items also cause problems, especially when you need the item on the bottom. The solution? Build slotted dividers from ½-inch plywood. If you wish, cut horizontal dadoes a bit oversize, wax the divider edges, and create an instant pull-out shelf.

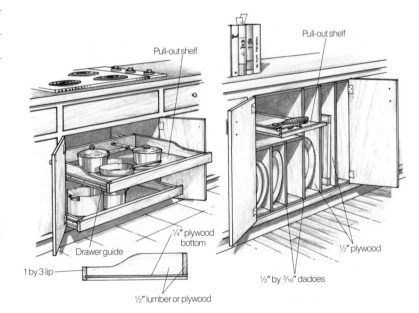

A Shelf System for Compact Discs

Here's an oak storage system for a burgeoning collection of compact discs.

To build it, round-over the top and bottom of one edge of a 1 by 8 long enough for all the shelves. Measure in $6\frac{3}{8}$ inches from the point where the rounding stops and rip the board to this width; cut it into 22-inch-long pieces. Cut a shallow groove for the bracket tips in the front of each shelf.

Round-over the edges of a 1 by 4, rip it into $1\frac{1}{2}$-inch-wide pieces, and cut them 22 inches long. Screw them to the back of the shelves. Then cut and assemble the shelf ends as shown.

To make each movable divider, nail and glue three scrap pieces together; then round-over the edges. Mount weatherstripping to the bottom piece as shown.

Fit shelf tracks inside grooves in 1 by 2 strips. Stain the wood; then finish with varnish or lacquer. Screw the tracks and mounting strips to studs.

Design: Bill Richter.

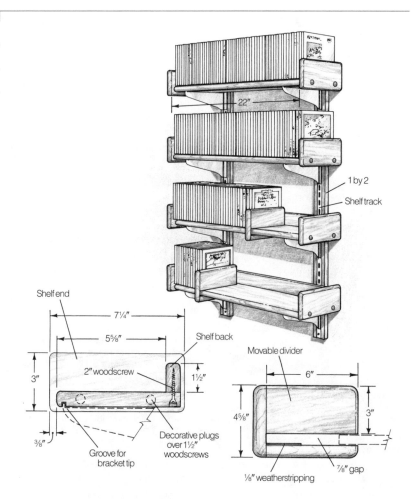

Shelf end

Shelf back

$7\frac{1}{4}$"

$5\frac{5}{8}$"

3"

2" woodscrew

$1\frac{1}{2}$"

$\frac{3}{8}$"

Groove for bracket tip

Decorative plugs over $1\frac{1}{2}$" woodscrews

22"

1 by 2

Shelf track

Movable divider

6"

$4\frac{5}{8}$"

3"

$\frac{1}{8}$" weatherstripping

$\frac{7}{8}$" gap

Audio & Video Cassette Racks

An extensive cassette collection deserves a home of its own.

To fashion an audio cassette rack, cut matching $\frac{3}{4}$- by $\frac{1}{4}$-inch dadoes in uprights; then incorporate them into a simple box or a larger cabinet frame as shown.

Thicker video cassettes require a wider slot, so it's easier to glue and nail thin molding strips to the uprights. Because video cassettes vary in size, measure yours carefully; then add $\frac{1}{16}$ inch to the slot width and another $\frac{1}{16}$ inch on each end when figuring the space between uprights.

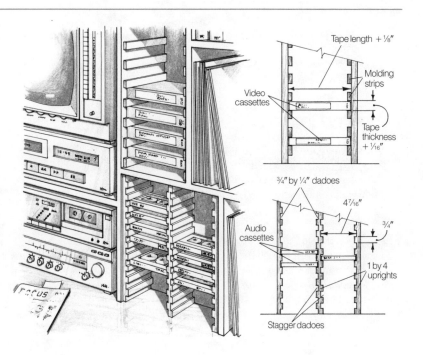

Tape length + $\frac{1}{8}$"

Molding strips

Video cassettes

Tape thickness + $\frac{1}{16}$"

$\frac{3}{4}$" by $\frac{1}{4}$" dadoes

$4\frac{7}{16}$"

$\frac{3}{4}$"

Audio cassettes

1 by 4 uprights

Stagger dadoes

Common Softwoods

Species	Characteristics
Cedars	
Alaska yellow	Pale yellow, bland wood that's heavy, strong, and very stable compared to other cedars. Very resistant to decay and splintering. Easily worked, but has a slightly unpleasant odor when cut. Limited availability; expensive.
Eastern red	Characterized by ivory sapwood and dark red heartwood. Highly aromatic (used in cedar chests and closet linings). Defect-prone but easily worked.
Incense	Ivory to russet western cedar. Soft and relatively weak, but versatile (used for pencil cladding). Can be quite knotty. Works easily; accepts glue and finishes well. Stable once dry and resistant to decay.
Northern / southern white	Less flamboyant in color and figure than western red. Soft and weak, but weathers well. Works easily. Not generally available in the West.
Port Orford	Pale yellow to brown in color with bland figure. Strong and dense with few defects. Works well and is stable. Hard to find, even in its native West.
Western red	Known for its handsome grain, color variation (ivory to pink, russet, and red), and resistance to decay. Soft and weak, but versatile. Works easily; takes glue and finishes well. Stable when dry. Widely available.
Cypress	Typically straight-grain wood in warm amber to red tones. Hard, strong, and moderately heavy with good decay resistance. Machines easily and shrinks little. Holds nails reasonably well. Often used in high-moisture areas (saunas, vats, greenhouses) as well as for sashwork and millwork. Good for food containers and utensils because it doesn't impart taste, odor, or color to food. Available largely in its native Southeast.
Douglas fir / western larch	Straight-grain amber woods with pronounced stripes. Low in resin and exceptionally strong and stiff. Often sold together (fir is predominant). Though highly valued for structural uses, quarter-sawn fir and larch produce beautiful vertical grain suitable for cabinets and millwork. Both work fairly well with sharp tools. Differences in grain density make heavily pigmented stains a poor choice.
Hemlocks / firs	
Eastern hemlock / balsam fir	Though coarse in texture, eastern hemlock (often sold with tamarack) is strong and free of resin. Balsam fir is similar, but less strong.
Western hemlock / true firs	Cream-colored, bland woods generally sold together as "Hem-fir" (firs include California red, grand, noble, Pacific silver, and subalpine—all western species). Light and moderately strong. Shrinkage and warping can be serious problems if wood isn't bone dry. Easily worked. Accepts glue, nails, and paint moderately well.
Pines	
Eastern white / western (Idaho white, lodgepole, Ponderosa, sugar)	Very white to russet. Soft and relatively weak; ideal woods for shaping. Smooth and uniform, though knots and pitch pockets are common. Little checking or warping. Hold fasteners moderately well with little splitting.
	Eastern white, Idaho white (sometimes called western white), and sugar: Favorites of pattern-makers because of their satiny surface and workability. *Lodgepole:* Straight-grain wood that comes in narrow widths; stable. Unlike other pines, its knots won't bleed through paint. *Ponderosa ("knotty pine"):* Versatile and popular.
Jack, red (Norway)	Bland in color and coarsely textured compared to most western pines or eastern white pine. Strong and moderately easy to work.
Southern yellow (shortleaf, longleaf, loblolly, slash, and pitch)	White to yellowish woods that are hard, strong, and moderately heavy. Generally coarse in texture and full of resin. Work and finish moderately well, but have excellent nail-holding ability. Prized for millwork is quarter-sawn heartwood of virgin longleaf pine.
Redwood	Red to russet and pink heartwood, creamy white sapwood. Heartwood is highly resistant to decay and insects. Lightweight but surprisingly strong. Quite soft (scratches, splinters, and dents easily). Produces wide, often clear, resin-free lumber. Works easily and finishes beautifully. Holds fasteners only moderately well and can be prone to splitting. Expensive outside the West.
Spruces	
Eastern	Nondescript, whitish wood that's uniform in grain. Relatively soft, but strong for its weight. Works easily, resists splitting, and takes paint and fasteners well. Remains stable.
Englemann	Similar to eastern spruce, but smoother in texture. Good for lightweight structural members and for exposed, painted surfaces.
Sitka	Creamy to pinkish brown, straight-grain wood that makes wide, clear lumber. Very strong for its weight. Works easily and planes to a silky sheen. Resists splintering.

Some Domestic & Exotic Hardwoods

Domestic species	Characteristics
Alder, red	Pinkish brown with little figure. Western states' utility wood often substituted for birch, but less hard and strong. Easy to work. Inexpensive.
Ash, white	Creamy to grayish brown, wide-grain wood that's tough and durable. Versatile; works easily and accepts finishes well. Moderately priced.
Basswood	Nondescript, creamy white to russet "woodcarver's wood." Lightweight, soft, and uniform in grain. Accepts glue and paint well; stable. Moderately priced.
Beech	Tan to reddish in color with conspicuous rays. Heavy and hard, but prone to checking and warping. Works fairly well; imparts no odor or taste. Moderately priced.
Birch, yellow	Light reddish brown with pleasing grain. Hard, heavy, and strong. Versatile; machines easily and accepts finishes well. Moderately priced.
Cherry, black	Uniform reddish brown color with some figure. Strong and hard but not heavy. Works well and takes a satiny finish; stable. Becomes red with age. Moderately priced.
Hickory/pecan	Reddish brown with uniform grain. Strong, hard woods that are often sold together. Must be seasoned carefully. Very tough and durable, yet easily worked. Moderately priced.
Maples, sugar and eastern	Reddish tan with great variety of grain (curly and bird's-eye are two types). Heavy, hard, and durable. Works easily and accepts finishes well; takes abuse. Moderately priced.
Oak, red	Very popular pinkish, fairly straight-grain wood with large pores. Heavy, hard, and very durable. Machines and finishes well. Moderately priced.
Oak, white	Yellowish brown in color with distinctive quarter-sawn rays and closed pores. Dense, strong, and very durable. Machines and finishes well. Moderately expensive.
Poplar, yellow	Yellowish brown to green wood with bland, uniform grain. Light and moderately soft. Works easily and shows no grain through paint; stable. Inexpensive.
Walnut, black	Chocolate brown wood with handsome grain and great figure variety. Durable and strong. Works well, takes high polish, and is very stable. Expensive.

Exotic species	Characteristics
Bocote	Brown to black wood (sometimes called Mexican rosewood) with yellow lines; straight to wavy grain. Heavy, hard, and oily. Expensive.
Cocobolo	Russet- to orange-colored Central and South American wood. Wavy grain and spicy aroma. Very hard, beautiful wood that may cause rash when worked. Expensive.
Ebonies, African and East Indian	African: Deep black with little figure. East Indian (Macassar): Brown to black with lighter streaks. Extremely hard and heavy woods that are difficult to find. Expensive.
Koa	Golden brown Hawaiian wood with some fiddleback figure. Soft, but finishes to a lustrous sheen. Becoming rare, but only moderately expensive.
Lauan	Tan to reddish "Philippine mahogany" with much ribbon grain and large pores. Softer, coarser, and stringier than true mahoganies; doesn't machine as well. Moderately priced.
Lignum vitae	Green to brown heartwood with light, swirling grain. Hard, heavy Caribbean wood that's difficult to work, extremely oily, but very durable. Expensive.
Mahoganies, African and Honduran	Golden reddish brown wood with variable grain and much figure. Moderately hard and very strong. Large, clear pieces available. Works very well. Moderately expensive.
Padouk	Golden red African wood often called vermilion. Uniform in grain and color (darkens to bronze); good for contrast. Hard, heavy wood that machines well. Expensive.
Purpleheart	Mildly striped wood (properly called amaranth) from American tropics; turns royal purple after cutting. Hard; works well. Moderately expensive.
Rosewoods, Brazilian and East Indian	Dark brown to violet and black with light and dark streaks. Brazilian has larger pores and is less stable than East Indian. Both finish beautifully. Expensive.
Satinwoods, East Indian and West Indian	Yellow to gold. Rare East Indian variety has great figure range, but checks easily. West Indian version is plainer, but more stable and workable. Both finish well. Expensive.
Teak	Golden brown Asian wood with some similarities to walnut. Very stable, even outdoors. Oily; sandy quality of wood hard on saw blades. Expensive.
Tulipwood	Pink to red and yellow Brazilian wood with wavy, irregular grain. Looks painted. Very hard; can be difficult to work. Expensive.
Zebrawood	Golden-hued African wood with pronounced black stripes and large pores. Lustrous when finished. Expensive.

INDEX